ABOUT THE AUTHOR

Frederick P. Brooks, Jr., is Professor and Chairman of the Computer Science Department at the University of North Carolina at Chapel Hill. He is best known as the "father of the IBM System/360," having served as project manager for its development and later as manager of the Operating System/360 software project during its design phase. Earlier, he was an architect of the IBM Stretch and Harvest computers.

At Chapel Hill, Dr. Brooks has participated in the establishment and guiding of the Triangle Universities Computation Center and the North Carolina Educational Computing Service. He has published *Automatic Data Processing,* the *System/360 Edition* of *Automatic Data Processing,* and chapters in several other books.

The Mythical Man-Month
Essays on Software Engineering

Frederick P. Brooks, Jr.
University of North Carolina, Chapel Hill

ADDISON-WESLEY PUBLISHING COMPANY

Reading, Massachusetts • Menlo Park, California
London • Amsterdam • Don Mills, Ontario • Sydney

Cover drawing: C. R. Knight, Mural of La Brea Tar Pits. Courtesy of the Photography Section of the Natural History Museum of Los Angeles County.

Reprinted with corrections, January 1982

ISBN 0-201-00650-2
RSTUVWX-AL-8987654

To two who especially enriched my IBM years:
Thomas J. Watson, Jr.,
whose deep concern for people still permeates his company,
and
Bob O. Evans,
whose bold leadership turned work into adventure.

Preface

In many ways, managing a large computer programming project is like managing any other large undertaking—in more ways than most programmers believe. But in many other ways it is different —in more ways than most professional managers expect.

The lore of the field is accumulating. There have been several conferences, sessions at AFIPS conferences, some books, and papers. But it is by no means yet in shape for any systematic textbook treatment. It seems appropriate, however, to offer this little book, reflecting essentially a personal view.

Although I originally grew up in the programming side of computer science, I was involved chiefly in hardware architecture during the years (1956–1963) that the autonomous control program and the high-level language compiler were developed. When in 1964 I became manager of Operating System/360, I found a programming world quite changed by the progress of the previous few years.

Managing OS/360 development was a very educational experience, albeit a very frustrating one. The team, including F. M. Trapnell who succeeded me as manager, has much to be proud of. The system contains many excellencies in design and execution, and it has been successful in achieving widespread use. Certain ideas, most noticeably device-independent input-output and external library management, were technical innovations now widely copied. It is now quite reliable, reasonably efficient, and very versatile.

The effort cannot be called wholly successful, however. Any OS/360 user is quickly aware of how much better it should be. The flaws in design and execution pervade especially the control program, as distinguished from the language compilers. Most of these flaws date from the 1964–65 design period and hence must be laid to my charge. Furthermore, the product was late, it took more memory than planned, the costs were several times the estimate, and it did not perform very well until several releases after the first.

After leaving IBM in 1965 to come to Chapel Hill as originally agreed when I took over OS/360, I began to analyze the OS/360 experience to see what management and technical lessons were to be learned. In particular, I wanted to explain the quite different management experiences encountered in System/360 hardware development and OS/360 software development. This book is a belated answer to Tom Watson's probing questions as to why programming is hard to manage.

In this quest I have profited from long conversations with R. P. Case, assistant manager 1964–65, and F. M. Trapnell, manager 1965–68. I have compared conclusions with other managers of jumbo programming projects, including F. J. Corbato of M.I.T., John Harr and V. Vyssotsky of Bell Telephone Laboratories, Charles Portman of International Computers Limited, A. P. Ershov of the Computation Laboratory of the Siberian Division, U.S.S.R. Academy of Sciences, and A. M. Pietrasanta of IBM.

My own conclusions are embodied in the essays that follow, which are intended for professional programmers, professional managers, and especially professional managers of programmers.

Although written as separable essays, there is a central argument contained especially in Chapters 2–7. Briefly, I believe that large programming projects suffer management problems different in kind from small ones, due to division of labor. I believe the critical need to be the preservation of the conceptual integrity of the product itself. These chapters explore both the difficulties of achieving this unity and methods for doing so. The later chapters explore other aspects of software engineering management.

The literature in this field is not abundant, but it is widely scattered. Hence I have tried to give references that will both illuminate particular points and guide the interested reader to other useful works. Many friends have read the manuscript, and some have prepared extensive helpful comments; where these seemed valuable but did not fit the flow of the text, I have included them in the notes.

Because this is a book of essays and not a text, all the references and notes have been banished to the end of the volume, and the reader is urged to ignore them on his first reading.

I am deeply indebted to Miss Sara Elizabeth Moore, Mr. David Wagner, and Mrs. Rebecca Burris for their help in preparing the manuscript, and to Professor Joseph C. Sloane for advice on illustration.

Chapel Hill, N.C.   F. P. B., Jr.
October 1974

Contents

1
The Tar Pit

1
The Tar Pit

Een schip op het strand is een baken in zee.
[*A ship on the beach is a lighthouse to the sea.*]

DUTCH PROVERB

C. R. Knight, Mural of La Brea Tar Pits
Photography Section, Natural History Museum of Los Angeles County

No scene from prehistory is quite so vivid as that of the mortal struggles of great beasts in the tar pits. In the mind's eye one sees dinosaurs, mammoths, and sabertoothed tigers struggling against the grip of the tar. The fiercer the struggle, the more entangling the tar, and no beast is so strong or so skillful but that he ultimately sinks.

Large-system programming has over the past decade been such a tar pit, and many great and powerful beasts have thrashed violently in it. Most have emerged with running systems—few have met goals, schedules, and budgets. Large and small, massive or wiry, team after team has become entangled in the tar. No one thing seems to cause the difficulty—any particular paw can be pulled away. But the accumulation of simultaneous and interacting factors brings slower and slower motion. Everyone seems to have been surprised by the stickiness of the problem, and it is hard to discern the nature of it. But we must try to understand it if we are to solve it.

Therefore let us begin by identifying the craft of system programming and the joys and woes inherent in it.

The Programming Systems Product

One occasionally reads newspaper accounts of how two programmers in a remodeled garage have built an important program that surpasses the best efforts of large teams. And every programmer is prepared to believe such tales, for he knows that he could build *any* program much faster than the 1000 statements/year reported for industrial teams.

Why then have not all industrial programming teams been replaced by dedicated garage duos? One must look at *what* is being produced.

In the upper left of Fig. 1.1 is a *program*. It is complete in itself, ready to be run by the author on the system on which it was developed. *That* is the thing commonly produced in garages, and

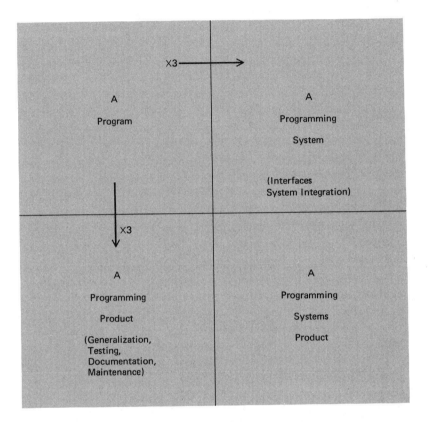

Fig. 1.1 Evolution of the programming systems product

that is the object the individual programmer uses in estimating productivity.

There are two ways a program can be converted into a more useful, but more costly, object. These two ways are represented by the boundaries in the diagram.

Moving down across the horizontal boundary, a program becomes a *programming product*. This is a program that can be run, tested, repaired, and extended by anybody. It is usable in many operating environments, for many sets of data. To become a generally usable programming product, a program must be written in a generalized fashion. In particular the range and form of inputs must be generalized as much as the basic algorithm will reasonably allow. Then the program must be thoroughly tested, so that it can be depended upon. This means that a substantial bank of test cases, exploring the input range and probing its boundaries, must be prepared, run, and recorded. Finally, promotion of a program to a programming product requires its thorough documentation, so that anyone may use it, fix it, and extend it. As a rule of thumb, I estimate that a programming product costs at least three times as much as a debugged program with the same function.

Moving across the vertical boundary, a program becomes a component in a *programming system.* This is a collection of interacting programs, coordinated in function and disciplined in format, so that the assemblage constitutes an entire facility for large tasks. To become a programming system component, a program must be written so that every input and output conforms in syntax and semantics with precisely defined interfaces. The program must also be designed so that it uses only a prescribed budget of resources—memory space, input-output devices, computer time. Finally, the program must be tested with other system components, in all expected combinations. This testing must be extensive, for the number of cases grows combinatorially. It is time-consuming, for subtle bugs arise from unexpected interactions of debugged components. A programming system component costs at least three times as much as a stand-alone program of the same function. The cost may be greater if the system has many components.

In the lower right-hand corner of Fig. 1.1 stands the *programming systems product.* This differs from the simple program in all of the above ways. It costs nine times as much. But it is the truly useful object, the intended product of most system programming efforts.

The Joys of the Craft

Why is programming fun? What delights may its practitioner expect as his reward?

First is the sheer joy of making things. As the child delights in his mud pie, so the adult enjoys building things, especially things of his own design. I think this delight must be an image of God's delight in making things, a delight shown in the distinctness and newness of each leaf and each snowflake.

Second is the pleasure of making things that are useful to other people. Deep within, we want others to use our work and to find it helpful. In this respect the programming system is not essentially different from the child's first clay pencil holder "for Daddy's office."

Third is the fascination of fashioning complex puzzle-like objects of interlocking moving parts and watching them work in subtle cycles, playing out the consequences of principles built in from the beginning. The programmed computer has all the fascination of the pinball machine or the jukebox mechanism, carried to the ultimate.

Fourth is the joy of always learning, which springs from the nonrepeating nature of the task. In one way or another the problem is ever new, and its solver learns something: sometimes practical, sometimes theoretical, and sometimes both.

Finally, there is the delight of working in such a tractable medium. The programmer, like the poet, works only slightly removed from pure thought-stuff. He builds his castles in the air, from air, creating by exertion of the imagination. Few media of creation are so flexible, so easy to polish and rework, so readily capable of realizing grand conceptual structures. (As we shall see later, this very tractability has its own problems.)

Yet the program construct, unlike the poet's words, is real in the sense that it moves and works, producing visible outputs separate from the construct itself. It prints results, draws pictures, produces sounds, moves arms. The magic of myth and legend has come true in our time. One types the correct incantation on a keyboard, and a display screen comes to life, showing things that never were nor could be.

Programming then is fun because it gratifies creative longings built deep within us and delights sensibilities we have in common with all men.

The Woes of the Craft

Not all is delight, however, and knowing the inherent woes makes it easier to bear them when they appear.

First, one must perform perfectly. The computer resembles the magic of legend in this respect, too. If one character, one pause, of the incantation is not strictly in proper form, the magic doesn't work. Human beings are not accustomed to being perfect, and few areas of human activity demand it. Adjusting to the requirement for perfection is, I think, the most difficult part of learning to program.[1]

Next, other people set one's objectives, provide one's resources, and furnish one's information. One rarely controls the circumstances of his work, or even its goal. In management terms, one's authority is not sufficient for his responsibility. It seems that in all fields, however, the jobs where things get done never have formal authority commensurate with responsibility. In practice, actual (as opposed to formal) authority is acquired from the very momentum of accomplishment.

The dependence upon others has a particular case that is especially painful for the system programmer. He depends upon other people's programs. These are often maldesigned, poorly implemented, incompletely delivered (no source code or test cases), and poorly documented. So he must spend hours studying and fixing things that in an ideal world would be complete, available, and usable.

The next woe is that designing grand concepts is fun; finding nitty little bugs is just work. With any creative activity come dreary hours of tedious, painstaking labor, and programming is no exception.

Next, one finds that debugging has a linear convergence, or worse, where one somehow expects a quadratic sort of approach to the end. So testing drags on and on, the last difficult bugs taking more time to find than the first.

The last woe, and sometimes the last straw, is that the product over which one has labored so long appears to be obsolete upon (or before) completion. Already colleagues and competitors are in hot pursuit of new and better ideas. Already the displacement of one's thought-child is not only conceived, but scheduled.

This always seems worse than it really is. The new and better product is generally not *available* when one completes his own; it is only talked about. It, too, will require months of development. The real tiger is never a match for the paper one, unless actual use is wanted. Then the virtues of reality have a satisfaction all their own.

Of course the technological base on which one builds is *always* advancing. As soon as one freezes a design, it becomes obsolete in terms of its concepts. But implementation of real products demands phasing and quantizing. The obsolescence of an implementation must be measured against other existing implementations, not against unrealized concepts. The challenge and the mission are to find real solutions to real problems on actual schedules with available resources.

This then is programming, both a tar pit in which many efforts have floundered and a creative activity with joys and woes all its own. For many, the joys far outweigh the woes, and for them the remainder of this book will attempt to lay some boardwalks across the tar.

2
The Mythical Man-Month

Restaurant Antoine

Fondé En 1840

AVIS AU PUBLIC

Faire de la bonne cuisine demande un certain temps. Si on vous fait attendre, c'est pour mieux vous servir, et vous plaire.

ENTREES (SUITE)

Côtelettes d'agneau grillées 2.50	Entrecôte marchand de vin 4.00
Côtelettes d'agneau aux champignons frais 2.75	Côtelettes d'agneau maison d'or 2.7
Filet de boeuf aux champignons frais 4.75	Côtelettes d'agneau à la parisienne 2.
Ris de veau à la financière 2.00	Fois de volaille à la brochette 1.50
Filet de boeuf nature 3.75	Tournedos nature 2.75
Tournedos Médicis 3.25	Filet de boeuf à la hawaïenne 4.00
Pigeonneaux sauce paradis 3.50	Tournedos à la hawaïenne 3.25
Tournedos sauce béarnaise 3.25	Tournedos marchand de vin 3.25
Entrecôte minute 2.75	Pigeonneaux grillés 3.00
Filet de boeuf béarnaise 4.00	Entrecôte nature 3.75
Tripes à la mode de Caen (commander d'avance) 2.00	Châteaubriand (30 minutes) 7.

LÉGUMES

Epinards sauce crême .60   Chou-fleur au gratin .60
Broccoli sauce hollandaise .80   Asperges fraîches au beurre .90
Pommes de terre au gratin .60   Carottes à la crème .60
Haricots verts au berre .60   Pommes de terre soufflées
Petits pois à la française .75

SALADES

Salade Antoine .60   Fonds d'artichauts Bayard .
Salade Mirabeau .75   Salade de laitue aux oeufs .60
Salade laitue au roquefort .80   Tomate frappée à la Jules César .60
Salade de laitue aux tomates .60   Salade de coeur de palmier 1.00
Salade de légumes .60   Salade aux pointes d'asperges .60
Salade d'anchois 1.00   Avocat à la vinaigrette .60

DESSERTS

Gâteau moka .50   Cerises jubilé 1.25
Méringue glacée .60   Crêpes à la gelée .80
Crêpes Suzette 1.25   Crêpes nature .70
Glace sauce chocolat .60   Omelette au rhum 1.10
Fruits de saison à l'eau-de-vie .75   Glace à la vanille .50
Omelette soufflée à la Jules César (2) 2.00   Fraises au kirsch
Omelette Alaska Antoine (2) 2.50   Pêche Melba .

FROMAGES

Roquefort .50   Liederkranz .50   Gruyère .50
Camembert .50   Fromage à la crême Philadelphie .50

CAFÉ ET THÉ

Café .20   Café au lait .20   Thé .20
Café brulôt diabolique 1.00   Thé glacé .20   Demi-tasse

EAUX MINERALES—BIERE—CIGARES—CIGARETTES

White Rock   Bière locale   Ciga
Vichy   Cliquot Club   Canada Dry   Cigarettes

Roy L. Alciatore, Propriétaire

713-717 Rue St. Louis   Nouvelle Orléans, Louisiane

2
The Mythical Man-Month

Good cooking takes time. If you are made to wait, it is to serve you better, and to please you.

MENU OF RESTAURANT ANTOINE, NEW ORLEANS

More software projects have gone awry for lack of calendar time than for all other causes combined. Why is this cause of disaster so common?

First, our techniques of estimating are poorly developed. More seriously, they reflect an unvoiced assumption which is quite untrue, i.e., that all will go well.

Second, our estimating techniques fallaciously confuse effort with progress, hiding the assumption that men and months are interchangeable.

Third, because we are uncertain of our estimates, software managers often lack the courteous stubbornness of Antoine's chef.

Fourth, schedule progress is poorly monitored. Techniques proven and routine in other engineering disciplines are considered radical innovations in software engineering.

Fifth, when schedule slippage is recognized, the natural (and traditional) response is to add manpower. Like dousing a fire with gasoline, this makes matters worse, much worse. More fire requires more gasoline, and thus begins a regenerative cycle which ends in disaster.

Schedule monitoring will be the subject of a separate essay. Let us consider other aspects of the problem in more detail.

Optimism

All programmers are optimists. Perhaps this modern sorcery especially attracts those who believe in happy endings and fairy godmothers. Perhaps the hundreds of nitty frustrations drive away all but those who habitually focus on the end goal. Perhaps it is merely that computers are young, programmers are younger, and the young are always optimists. But however the selection process works, the result is indisputable: "This time it will surely run," or "I just found the last bug."

So the first false assumption that underlies the scheduling of systems programming is that *all will go well,* i.e., that *each task will take only as long as it "ought" to take.*

The pervasiveness of optimism among programmers deserves more than a flip analysis. Dorothy Sayers, in her excellent book, *The Mind of the Maker,* divides creative activity into three stages: the idea, the implementation, and the interaction. A book, then, or a computer, or a program comes into existence first as an ideal construct, built outside time and space, but complete in the mind of the author. It is realized in time and space, by pen, ink, and paper, or by wire, silicon, and ferrite. The creation is complete when someone reads the book, uses the computer, or runs the program, thereby interacting with the mind of the maker.

This description, which Miss Sayers uses to illuminate not only human creative activity but also the Christian doctrine of the Trinity, will help us in our present task. For the human makers of things, the incompletenesses and inconsistencies of our ideas become clear only during implementation. Thus it is that writing, experimentation, "working out" are essential disciplines for the theoretician.

In many creative activities the medium of execution is intractable. Lumber splits; paints smear; electrical circuits ring. These physical limitations of the medium constrain the ideas that may be expressed, and they also create unexpected difficulties in the implementation.

Implementation, then, takes time and sweat both because of the physical media and because of the inadequacies of the underlying ideas. We tend to blame the physical media for most of our implementation difficulties; for the media are not "ours" in the way the ideas are, and our pride colors our judgment.

Computer programming, however, creates with an exceedingly tractable medium. The programmer builds from pure thought-stuff: concepts and very flexible representations thereof. Because the medium is tractable, we expect few difficulties in implementation; hence our pervasive optimism. Because our ideas are faulty, we have bugs; hence our optimism is unjustified.

In a single task, the assumption that all will go well has a probabilistic effect on the schedule. It might indeed go as planned, for there is a probability distribution for the delay that will be encountered, and "no delay" has a finite probability. A large programming effort, however, consists of many tasks, some chained end-to-end. The probability that each will go well becomes vanishingly small.

The Man-Month

The second fallacious thought mode is expressed in the very unit of effort used in estimating and scheduling: the man-month. Cost does indeed vary as the product of the number of men and the number of months. Progress does not. *Hence the man-month as a unit for measuring the size of a job is a dangerous and deceptive myth.* It implies that men and months are interchangeable.

Men and months are interchangeable commodities only when a task can be partitioned among many workers *with no communication among them* (Fig. 2.1). This is true of reaping wheat or picking cotton; it is not even approximately true of systems programming.

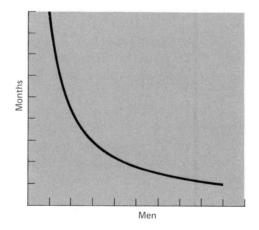

Fig. 2.1 Time versus number of workers—perfectly partitionable task

When a task cannot be partitioned because of sequential constraints, the application of more effort has no effect on the schedule (Fig. 2.2). The bearing of a child takes nine months, no matter
how many women are assigned. Many software tasks have this
characteristic because of the sequential nature of debugging.

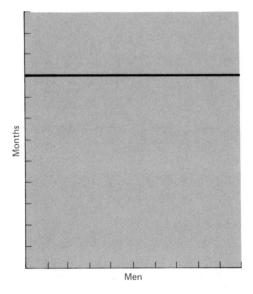

Fig. 2.2   Time versus number of workers—unpartitionable task

In tasks that can be partitioned but which require communication among the subtasks, the effort of communication must be
added to the amount of work to be done. Therefore the best that
can be done is somewhat poorer than an even trade of men for
months (Fig. 2.3).

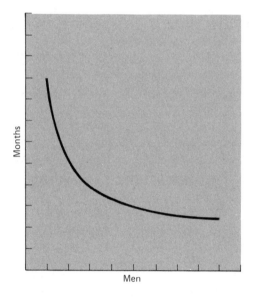

Fig. 2.3 Time versus number of workers—partitionable task requiring communication

The added burden of communication is made up of two parts, training and intercommunication. Each worker must be trained in the technology, the goals of the effort, the overall strategy, and the plan of work. This training cannot be partitioned, so this part of the added effort varies linearly with the number of workers.[1]

Intercommunication is worse. If each part of the task must be separately coordinated with each other part, the effort increases as $n(n-1)/2$. Three workers require three times as much pairwise intercommunication as two; four require six times as much as two. If, moreover, there need to be conferences among three, four, etc., workers to resolve things jointly, matters get worse yet. The added effort of communicating may fully counteract the division of the original task and bring us to the situation of Fig. 2.4.

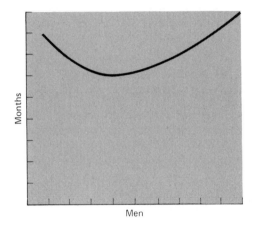

Fig. 2.4 Time versus number of workers—task with complex interrelationships

Since software construction is inherently a systems effort—an exercise in complex interrelationships—communication effort is great, and it quickly dominates the decrease in individual task time brought about by partitioning. Adding more men then lengthens, not shortens, the schedule.

Systems Test

No parts of the schedule are so thoroughly affected by sequential constraints as component debugging and system test. Furthermore, the time required depends on the number and subtlety of the errors encountered. Theoretically this number should be zero. Because of optimism, we usually expect the number of bugs to be smaller than it turns out to be. Therefore testing is usually the most mis-scheduled part of programming.

For some years I have been successfully using the following rule of thumb for scheduling a software task:

$\frac{1}{3}$ planning
$\frac{1}{6}$ coding
$\frac{1}{4}$ component test and early system test
$\frac{1}{4}$ system test, all components in hand.

This differs from conventional scheduling in several important ways:

1. The fraction devoted to planning is larger than normal. Even so, it is barely enough to produce a detailed and solid specification, and not enough to include research or exploration of totally new techniques.
2. The *half* of the schedule devoted to debugging of completed code is much larger than normal.
3. The part that is easy to estimate, i.e., coding, is given only one-sixth of the schedule.

In examining conventionally scheduled projects, I have found that few allowed one-half of the projected schedule for testing, but that most did indeed spend half of the actual schedule for that purpose. Many of these were on schedule until and except in system testing.[2]

Failure to allow enough time for system test, in particular, is peculiarly disastrous. Since the delay comes at the end of the schedule, no one is aware of schedule trouble until almost the delivery date. Bad news, late and without warning, is unsettling to customers and to managers.

Furthermore, delay at this point has unusually severe financial, as well as psychological, repercussions. The project is fully staffed, and cost-per-day is maximum. More seriously, the software is to support other business effort (shipping of computers, operation of new facilities, etc.) and the secondary costs of delaying these are very high, for it is almost time for software shipment.

Indeed, these secondary costs may far outweigh all others. It is therefore very important to allow enough system test time in the original schedule.

Gutless Estimating

Observe that for the programmer, as for the chef, the urgency of the patron may govern the scheduled completion of the task, but it cannot govern the actual completion. An omelette, promised in two minutes, may appear to be progressing nicely. But when it has not set in two minutes, the customer has two choices—wait or eat it raw. Software customers have had the same choices.

The cook has another choice; he can turn up the heat. The result is often an omelette nothing can save—burned in one part, raw in another.

Now I do not think software managers have less inherent courage and firmness than chefs, nor than other engineering managers. But false scheduling to match the patron's desired date is much more common in our discipline than elsewhere in engineering. It is very difficult to make a vigorous, plausible, and job-risking defense of an estimate that is derived by no quantitative method, supported by little data, and certified chiefly by the hunches of the managers.

Clearly two solutions are needed. We need to develop and publicize productivity figures, bug-incidence figures, estimating rules, and so on. The whole profession can only profit from sharing such data.

Until estimating is on a sounder basis, individual managers will need to stiffen their backbones and defend their estimates with the assurance that their poor hunches are better than wish-derived estimates.

Regenerative Schedule Disaster

What does one do when an essential software project is behind schedule? Add manpower, naturally. As Figs. 2.1 through 2.4 suggest, this may or may not help.

Let us consider an example.[3] Suppose a task is estimated at 12 man-months and assigned to three men for four months, and that there are measurable mileposts A, B, C, D, which are scheduled to fall at the end of each month (Fig. 2.5).

Now suppose the first milepost is not reached until two months have elapsed (Fig. 2.6). What are the alternatives facing the manager?

1. Assume that the task must be done on time. Assume that only the first part of the task was misestimated, so Fig. 2.6 tells the story accurately. Then 9 man-months of effort remain, and two months, so 4½ men will be needed. Add 2 men to the 3 assigned.

2. Assume that the task must be done on time. Assume that the whole estimate was uniformly low, so that Fig. 2.7 really describes the situation. Then 18 man-months of effort remain, and two months, so 9 men will be needed. Add 6 men to the 3 assigned.

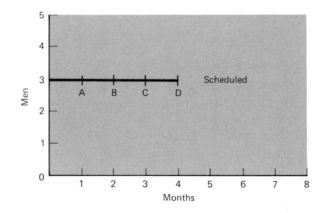

Figure 2.5

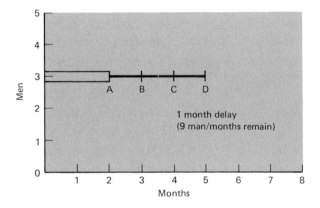

Figure 2.6

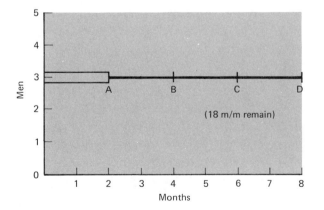

Figure 2.7

3. Reschedule. I like the advice given by P. Fagg, an experienced hardware engineer, "Take no small slips." That is, allow enough time in the new schedule to ensure that the work can be carefully and thoroughly done, and that rescheduling will not have to be done again.

4. Trim the task. In practice this tends to happen anyway, once the team observes schedule slippage. Where the secondary costs of delay are very high, this is the only feasible action. The manager's only alternatives are to trim it formally and carefully, to reschedule, or to watch the task get silently trimmed by hasty design and incomplete testing.

In the first two cases, insisting that the unaltered task be completed in four months is disastrous. Consider the regenerative effects, for example, for the first alternative (Fig. 2.8). The two new men, however competent and however quickly recruited, will require training in the task by one of the experienced men. If this takes a month, *3 man-months will have been devoted to work not in the original estimate.* Furthermore, the task, originally partitioned three ways, must be repartitioned into five parts; hence some work already done will be lost, and system testing must be lengthened. So at the end of the third month, substantially more than 7 man-months of effort remain, and 5 trained people and one month are available. As Fig. 2.8 suggests, the product is just as late as if no one had been added (Fig. 2.6).

To hope to get done in four months, considering only training time and not repartitioning and extra systems test, would require adding 4 men, not 2, at the end of the second month. To cover repartitioning and system test effects, one would have to add still other men. Now, however, one has at least a 7-man team, not a 3-man one; thus such aspects as team organization and task division are different in kind, not merely in degree.

Notice that by the end of the third month things look very black. The March 1 milestone has not been reached in spite of all

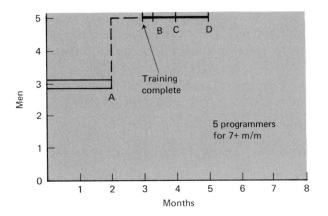

Figure 2.8

the managerial effort. The temptation is very strong to repeat the cycle, adding yet more manpower. Therein lies madness.

The foregoing assumed that only the first milestone was misestimated. If on March 1 one makes the conservative assumption that the whole schedule was optimistic, as Fig. 2.7 depicts, one wants to add 6 men just to the original task. Calculation of the training, repartitioning, system testing effects is left as an exercise for the reader. Without a doubt, the regenerative disaster will yield a poorer product, later, than would rescheduling with the original three men, unaugmented.

Oversimplifying outrageously, we state Brooks's Law:

Adding manpower to a late software project makes it later.

This then is the demythologizing of the man-month. The number of months of a project depends upon its sequential constraints. The maximum number of men depends upon the number of independent subtasks. From these two quantities one can derive schedules using fewer men and more months. (The only risk is product obsolescence.) One cannot, however, get workable schedules using more men and fewer months. More software projects have gone awry for lack of calendar time than for all other causes combined.

3
The Surgical Team

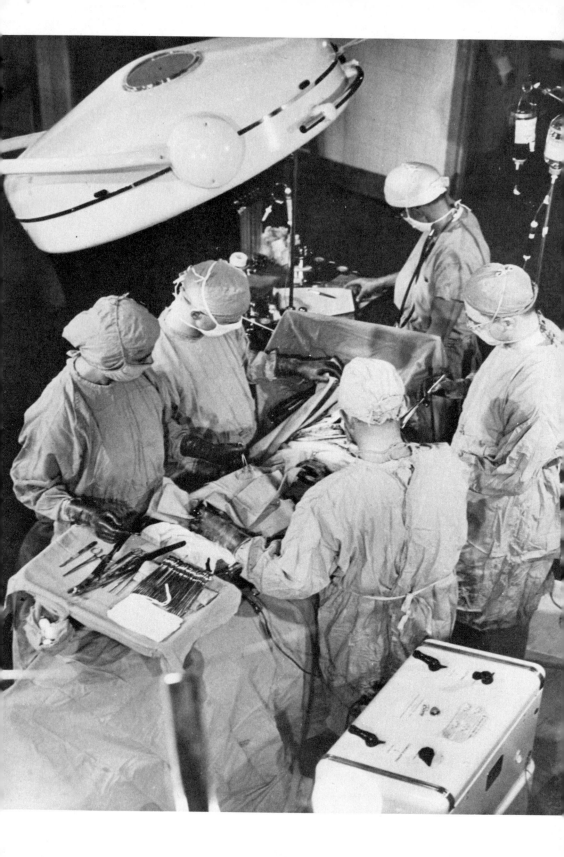

3
The Surgical Team

These studies revealed large individual differences between high and low performers, often by an order of magnitude.

SACKMAN, ERIKSON, AND GRANT[1]

UPI Photo

At computer society meetings one continually hears young programming managers assert that they favor a small, sharp team of first-class people, rather than a project with hundreds of programmers, and those by implication mediocre. So do we all.

But this naive statement of the alternatives avoids the hard problem—how does one build *large* systems on a meaningful schedule? Let us look at each side of this question in more detail.

The Problem

Programming managers have long recognized wide productivity variations between good programmers and poor ones. But the actual measured magnitudes have astounded all of us. In one of their studies, Sackman, Erikson, and Grant were measuring performances of a group of experienced programmers. Within just this group the ratios between best and worst performances averaged about 10:1 on productivity measurements and an amazing 5:1 on program speed and space measurements! In short the $20,000/year programmer may well be 10 times as productive as the $10,000/year one. The converse may be true, too. The data showed no correlation whatsoever between experience and performance. (I doubt if that is universally true.)

I have earlier argued that the sheer number of minds to be coordinated affects the cost of the effort, for a major part of the cost is communication and correcting the ill effects of miscommunication (system debugging). This, too, suggests that one wants the system to be built by as few minds as possible. Indeed, most experience with large programming systems shows that the brute-force approach is costly, slow, inefficient, and produces systems that are not conceptually integrated. OS/360, Exec 8, Scope 6600, Multics, TSS, SAGE, etc.—the list goes on and on.

The conclusion is simple: if a 200-man project has 25 managers who are the most competent and experienced programmers, fire the 175 troops and put the managers back to programming.

Now let's examine this solution. On the one hand, it fails to approach the ideal of the *small* sharp team, which by common consensus shouldn't exceed 10 people. It is so large that it will need to have at least two levels of management, or about five managers. It will additionally need support in finance, personnel, space, secretaries, and machine operators.

On the other hand, the original 200-man team was not large enough to build the really large systems by brute-force methods. Consider OS/360, for example. At the peak over 1000 people were working on it—programmers, writers, machine operators, clerks, secretaries, managers, support groups, and so on. From 1963 through 1966 probably 5000 man-years went into its design, construction, and documentation. Our postulated 200-man team would have taken 25 years to have brought the product to its present stage, if men and months traded evenly!

This then is the problem with the small, sharp team concept: *it is too slow for really big systems.* Consider the OS/360 job as it might be tackled with a small, sharp team. Postulate a 10-man team. As a bound, let them be seven times as productive as mediocre programmers in both programming and documentation, because they are sharp. Assume OS/360 was built only by mediocre programmers (which is *far* from the truth). As a bound, assume that another productivity improvement factor of seven comes from reduced communication on the part of the smaller team. Assume the *same* team stays on the entire job. Well, $5000/(10 \times 7 \times 7) = 10$; they can do the 5000 man-year job in 10 years. Will the product be interesting 10 years after its initial design? Or will it have been made obsolete by the rapidly developing software technology?

The dilemma is a cruel one. For efficiency and conceptual integrity, one prefers a few good minds doing design and construction. Yet for large systems one wants a way to bring considerable manpower to bear, so that the product can make a timely appearance. How can these two needs be reconciled?

Mills's Proposal

A proposal by Harlan Mills offers a fresh and creative solution.[2,3] Mills proposes that each segment of a large job be tackled by a team, but that the team be organized like a surgical team rather than a hog-butchering team. That is, instead of each member cutting away on the problem, one does the cutting and the others give him every support that will enhance his effectiveness and productivity.

A little thought shows that this concept meets the desiderata, if it can be made to work. Few minds are involved in design and construction, yet many hands are brought to bear. Can it work? Who are the anesthesiologists and nurses on a programming team, and how is the work divided? Let me freely mix metaphors to suggest how such a team might work if enlarged to include all conceivable support.

The surgeon. Mills calls him a *chief programmer*. He personally defines the functional and performance specifications, designs the program, codes it, tests it, and writes its documentation. He writes in a structured programming language such as PL/I, and has effective access to a computing system which not only runs his tests but also stores the various versions of his programs, allows easy file updating, and provides text editing for his documentation. He needs great talent, ten years experience, and considerable systems and application knowledge, whether in applied mathematics, business data handling, or whatever.

The copilot. He is the alter ego of the surgeon, able to do any part of the job, but is less experienced. His main function is to share in the design as a thinker, discussant, and evaluator. The surgeon tries ideas on him, but is not bound by his advice. The copilot often represents his team in discussions of function and interface with other teams. He knows all the code intimately. He researches alternative design strategies. He obviously serves as insurance against disaster to the surgeon. He may even write code, but he is not responsible for any part of the code.

The administrator. The surgeon is boss, and he must have the last word on personnel, raises, space, and so on, but he must spend almost none of his time on these matters. Thus he needs a professional administrator who handles money, people, space, and machines, and who interfaces with the administrative machinery of the rest of the organization. Baker suggests that the administrator has a full-time job only if the project has substantial legal, contractual, reporting, or financial requirements because of the user-producer relationship. Otherwise, one administrator can serve two teams.

The editor. The surgeon is responsible for generating the documentation—for maximum clarity he must write it. This is true of both external and internal descriptions. The editor, however, takes the draft or dictated manuscript produced by the surgeon and criticizes it, reworks it, provides it with references and bibliography, nurses it through several versions, and oversees the mechanics of production.

Two secretaries. The administrator and the editor will each need a secretary; the administrator's secretary will handle project correspondence and non-product files.

The program clerk. He is responsible for maintaining all the technical records of the team in a programming-product library. The clerk is trained as a secretary and has responsibility for both machine-readable and human-readable files.

All computer input goes to the clerk, who logs and keys it if required. The output listings go back to him to be filed and indexed. The most recent runs of any model are kept in a status notebook; all previous ones are filed in a chronological archive.

Absolutely vital to Mills's concept is the transformation of programming "from private art to public practice" by making *all* the computer runs visible to all team members and identifying all programs and data as team property, not private property.

The specialized function of the program clerk relieves programmers of clerical chores, systematizes and ensures proper performance of those oft-neglected chores, and enhances the team's most valuable asset—its work-product. Clearly the concept as set forth above assumes batch runs. When interactive terminals are used, particularly those with no hard-copy output, the program clerk's functions do not diminish, but they change. Now he logs all updates of team program copies from private working copies, still handles all batch runs, and uses his own interactive facility to control the integrity and availability of the growing product.

The toolsmith.   File-editing, text-editing, and interactive debugging services are now readily available, so that a team will rarely need its own machine and machine-operating crew. But these services must be available with unquestionably satisfactory response and reliability; and the surgeon must be sole judge of the adequacy of the service available to him. He needs a toolsmith, responsible for ensuring this adequacy of the basic service and for constructing, maintaining, and upgrading special tools—mostly interactive computer services—needed by his team. Each team will need its own toolsmith, regardless of the excellence and reliability of any centrally provided service, for his job is to see to the tools needed or wanted by *his* surgeon, without regard to any other team's needs. The tool-builder will often construct specialized utilities, catalogued procedures, macro libraries.

The tester.   The surgeon will need a bank of suitable test cases for testing pieces of his work as he writes it, and then for testing the whole thing. The tester is therefore both an adversary who devises system test cases from the functional specs, and an assistant who devises test data for the day-by-day debugging. He would also plan testing sequences and set up the scaffolding required for component tests.

The language lawyer.   By the time Algol came along, people began to recognize that most computer installations have one or two people who delight in mastery of the intricacies of a programming language. And these experts turn out to be very useful and very widely consulted. The talent here is rather different from that of the surgeon, who is primarily a system designer and who thinks representations. The language lawyer can find a neat and efficient way to use the language to do difficult, obscure, or tricky things. Often he will need to do small studies (two or three days) on good technique. One language lawyer can service two or three surgeons.

This, then, is how 10 people might contribute in well-differentiated and specialized roles on a programming team built on the surgical model.

How It Works

The team just defined meets the desiderata in several ways. Ten people, seven of them professionals, are at work on the problem, but the system is the product of one mind—or at most two, acting *uno animo.*

Notice in particular the differences between a team of two programmers conventionally organized and the surgeon-copilot team. First, in the conventional team the partners divide the work, and each is responsible for design and implementation of part of the work. In the surgical team, the surgeon and copilot are each cognizant of all of the design and all of the code. This saves the labor of allocating space, disk accesses, etc. It also ensures the conceptual integrity of the work.

Second, in the conventional team the partners are equal, and the inevitable differences of judgment must be talked out or compromised. Since the work and resources are divided, the differences in judgment are confined to overall strategy and interfacing, but they are compounded by differences of interest—e.g., whose space will be used for a buffer. In the surgical team, there are no differences of interest, and differences of judgment are settled by the surgeon unilaterally. These two differences—lack of division of the problem and the superior-subordinate relationship—make it possible for the surgical team to act *uno animo.*

Yet the specialization of function of the remainder of the team is the key to its efficiency, for it permits a radically simpler communication pattern among the members, as Fig. 3.1 shows.

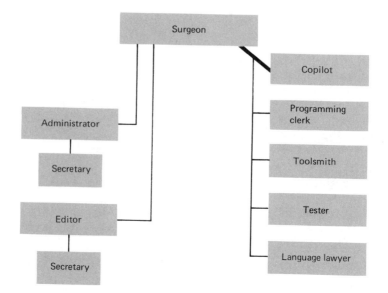

Fig. 3.1 Communication patterns in 10-man programming teams

Baker's article[3] reports on a single, small-scale test of the team concept. It worked as predicted for that case, with phenomenally good results.

Scaling Up

So far, so good. The problem, however, is how to build things that today take 5000 man-years, not things that take 20 or 30. A 10-man team can be effective no matter how it is organized, if the *whole* job is within its purview. But how is the surgical team concept to be used on large jobs when several hundred people are brought to bear on the task?

The success of the scaling-up process depends upon the fact that the conceptual integrity of each piece has been radically improved—that the number of minds determining the design has been divided by seven. So it is possible to put 200 people on a problem and face the problem of coordinating only 20 minds, those of the surgeons.

For that coordination problem, however, separate techniques must be used, and these are discussed in succeeding chapters. Let it suffice here to say that the entire system also must have conceptual integrity, and that requires a system architect to design it all, from the top down. To make that job manageable, a sharp distinction must be made between architecture and implementation, and the system architect must confine himself scrupulously to architecture. However, such roles and techniques have been shown to be feasible and, indeed, very productive.

4
Aristocracy, Democracy, and System Design

4
Aristocracy, Democracy, and System Design

This great church is an incomparable work of art. There is neither aridity nor confusion in the tenets it sets forth. . . .

It is the zenith of a style, the work of artists who had understood and assimilated all their predecessors' successes, in complete possession of the techniques of their times, but using them without indiscreet display nor gratuitous feats of skill.

It was Jean d'Orbais who undoubtedly conceived the general plan of the building, a plan which was respected, at least in its essential elements, by his successors. This is one of the reasons for the extreme coherence and unity of the edifice.

REIMS CATHEDRAL GUIDEBOOK[1]

Photographies Emmanuel Boudot-Lamotte

Conceptual Integrity

Most European cathedrals show differences in plan or architectural style between parts built in different generations by different builders. The later builders were tempted to "improve" upon the designs of the earlier ones, to reflect both changes in fashion and differences in individual taste. So the peaceful Norman transept abuts and contradicts the soaring Gothic nave, and the result proclaims the pridefulness of the builders as much as the glory of God.

Against these, the architectural unity of Reims stands in glorious contrast. The joy that stirs the beholder comes as much from the integrity of the design as from any particular excellences. As the guidebook tells, this integrity was achieved by the self-abnegation of eight generations of builders, each of whom sacrificed some of his ideas so that the whole might be of pure design. The result proclaims not only the glory of God, but also His power to salvage fallen men from their pride.

Even though they have not taken centuries to build, most programming systems reflect conceptual disunity far worse than that of cathedrals. Usually this arises not from a serial succession of master designers, but from the separation of design into many tasks done by many men.

I will contend that conceptual integrity is *the* most important consideration in system design. It is better to have a system omit certain anomalous features and improvements, but to reflect one set of design ideas, than to have one that contains many good but independent and uncoordinated ideas. In this chapter and the next two, we will examine the consequences of this theme for programming system design:

- How is conceptual integrity to be achieved?
- Does not this argument imply an elite, or aristocracy of architects, and a horde of plebeian implementers whose creative talents and ideas are suppressed?

- How does one keep the architects from drifting off into the blue with unimplementable or costly specifications?
- How does one ensure that every trifling detail of an architectural specification gets communicated to the implementer, properly understood by him, and accurately incorporated into the product?

Achieving Conceptual Integrity

The purpose of a programming system is to make a computer easy to use. To do this, it furnishes languages and various facilities that are in fact programs invoked and controlled by language features. But these facilities are bought at a price: the external description of a programming system is ten to twenty times as large as the external description of the computer system itself. The user finds it far easier to specify any particular function, but there are far more to choose from, and far more options and formats to remember.

Ease of use is enhanced only if the time gained in functional specification exceeds the time lost in learning, remembering, and searching manuals. With modern programming systems this gain does exceed the cost, but in recent years the ratio of gain to cost seems to have fallen as more and more complex functions have been added. I am haunted by the memory of the ease of use of the IBM 650, even without an assembler or any other software at all.

Because ease of use is the purpose, this ratio of function to conceptual complexity is the ultimate test of system design. Neither function alone nor simplicity alone defines a good design.

This point is widely misunderstood. Operating System/360 is hailed by its builders as the finest ever built, because it indisputably has the most function. Function, and not simplicity, has always been the measure of excellence for its designers. On the other hand, the Time-Sharing System for the PDP-10 is hailed by its builders as the finest, because of its simplicity and the spareness of its concepts. By any measure, however, its function is not even in the same class as that of OS/360. As soon as ease of use is held up as the criterion, each of these is seen to be unbalanced, reaching for only half of the true goal.

For a given level of function, however, that system is best in which one can specify things with the most simplicity and straightforwardness. *Simplicity* is not enough. Mooers's TRAC language and Algol 68 achieve simplicity as measured by the number of distinct elementary concepts. They are not, however, *straightforward.* The expression of the things one wants to do often requires involuted and unexpected combinations of the basic facilities. It is not enough to learn the elements and rules of combination; one must also learn the idiomatic usage, a whole lore of how the elements are combined in practice. Simplicity and straightforwardness proceed from conceptual integrity. Every part must reflect the same philosophies and the same balancing of desiderata. Every part must even use the same techniques in syntax and analogous notions in semantics. Ease of use, then, dictates unity of design, conceptual integrity.

Aristocracy and Democracy

Conceptual integrity in turn dictates that the design must proceed from one mind, or from a very small number of agreeing resonant minds.

Schedule pressures, however, dictate that system building needs many hands. Two techniques are available for resolving this dilemma. The first is a careful division of labor between architecture and implementation. The second is the new way of structuring programming implementation teams discussed in the previous chapter.

The separation of architectural effort from implementation is a very powerful way of getting conceptual integrity on very large projects. I myself have seen it used with great success on IBM's Stretch computer and on the System/360 computer product line.

I have seen it fail through lack of application on Operating System/360.

By the *architecture* of a system, I mean the complete and detailed specification of the user interface. For a computer this is the programming manual. For a compiler it is the language manual. For a control program it is the manuals for the language or languages used to invoke its functions. For the entire system it is the union of the manuals the user must consult to do his entire job.

The architect of a system, like the architect of a building, is the user's agent. It is his job to bring professional and technical knowledge to bear in the unalloyed interest of the user, as opposed to the interests of the salesman, the fabricator, etc.[2]

Architecture must be carefully distinguished from implementation. As Blaauw has said, "Where architecture tells *what* happens, implementation tells *how* it is made to happen."[3] He gives as a simple example a clock, whose architecture consists of the face, the hands, and the winding knob. When a child has learned this architecture, he can tell time as easily from a wristwatch as from a church tower. The implementation, however, and its realization, describe what goes on inside the case—powering by any of many mechanisms and accuracy control by any of many.

In System/360, for example, a single computer architecture is implemented quite differently in each of some nine models. Conversely, a single implementation, the Model 30 data flow, memory, and microcode, serves at different times for four different architectures: a System/360 computer, a multiplex channel with up to 224 logically independent subchannels, a selector channel, and a 1401 computer.[4]

The same distinction is equally applicable to programming systems. There is a U.S. standard Fortran IV. This is the architecture for many compilers. Within this architecture many implementations are possible: text-in-core or compiler-in-core, fast-compile or optimizing, syntax-directed or *ad-hoc*. Likewise any assembler language or job-control language admits of many implementations of the assembler or scheduler.

Now we can deal with the deeply emotional question of aristocracy versus democracy. Are not the architects a new aristocracy, an intellectual elite, set up to tell the poor dumb implementers what to do? Has not all the creative work been sequestered for this elite, leaving the implementers as cogs in the machine? Won't one get a better product by getting the good ideas from all the team, following a democratic philosophy, rather than by restricting the development of specifications to a few?

As to the last question, it is the easiest. I will certainly not contend that only the architects will have good architectural ideas. Often the fresh concept does come from an implementer or from a user. However, all my own experience convinces me, and I have tried to show, that the conceptual integrity of a system determines its ease of use. Good features and ideas that do not integrate with a system's basic concepts are best left out. If there appear many such important but incompatible ideas, one scraps the whole system and starts again on an integrated system with different basic concepts.

As to the aristocracy charge, the answer must be yes and no. Yes, in the sense that there must be few architects, their product must endure longer than that of an implementer, and the architect sits at the focus of forces which he must ultimately resolve in the user's interest. If a system is to have conceptual integrity, someone must control the concepts. That is an aristocracy that needs no apology.

No, because the setting of external specifications is not more creative work than the designing of implementations. It is just different creative work. The design of an implementation, given an architecture, requires and allows as much design creativity, as many new ideas, and as much technical brilliance as the design of the external specifications. Indeed, the cost-performance ratio of the product will depend most heavily on the implementer, just as ease of use depends most heavily on the architect.

There are many examples from other arts and crafts that lead one to believe that discipline is good for art. Indeed, an artist's aphorism asserts, "Form is liberating." The worst buildings are those whose budget was too great for the purposes to be served. Bach's creative output hardly seems to have been squelched by the necessity of producing a limited-form cantata each week. I am sure that the Stretch computer would have had a better architecture had it been more tightly constrained; the constraints imposed by the System/360 Model 30's budget were in my opinion entirely beneficial for the Model 75's architecture.

Similarly, I observe that the external provision of an architecture enhances, not cramps, the creative style of an implementing group. They focus at once on the part of the problem no one has addressed, and inventions begin to flow. In an unconstrained implementing group, most thought and debate goes into architectural decisions, and implementation proper gets short shrift.[5]

This effect, which I have seen many times, is confirmed by R. W. Conway, whose group at Cornell built the PL/C compiler for the PL/I language. He says, "We finally decided to implement the language unchanged and unimproved, for the debates about language would have taken all our effort."[6]

What Does the Implementer Do While Waiting?

It is a very humbling experience to make a multimillion-dollar mistake, but it is also very memorable. I vividly recall the night we decided how to organize the actual writing of external specifications for OS/360. The manager of architecture, the manager of control program implementation, and I were threshing out the plan, schedule, and division of responsibilities.

The architecture manager had 10 good men. He asserted that they could write the specifications and do it right. It would take ten months, three more than the schedule allowed.

The control program manager had 150 men. He asserted that they could prepare the specifications, with the architecture team coordinating; it would be well-done and practical, and he could do it on schedule. Furthermore, if the architecture team did it, his 150 men would sit twiddling their thumbs for ten months.

To this the architecture manager responded that if I gave the control program team the responsibility, the result would *not* in fact be on time, but would also be three months late, and of much lower quality. I did, and it was. He was right on both counts. Moreover, the lack of conceptual integrity made the system far more costly to build and change, and I would estimate that it added a year to debugging time.

Many factors, of course, entered into that mistaken decision; but the overwhelming one was schedule time and the appeal of putting all those 150 implementers to work. It is this siren song whose deadly hazards I would now make visible.

When it is proposed that a small architecture team in fact write all the external specifications for a computer or a programming system, the implementers raise three objections:

- The specifications will be too rich in function and will not reflect practical cost considerations.
- The architects will get all the creative fun and shut out the inventiveness of the implementers.
- The many implementers will have to sit idly by while the specifications come through the narrow funnel that is the architecture team.

The first of these is a real danger, and it will be treated in the next chapter. The other two are illusions, pure and simple. As we have seen above, implementation is also a creative activity of the first order. The opportunity to be creative and inventive in implementation is not significantly diminished by working within a given external specification, and the order of creativity may even be enhanced by that discipline. The total product will surely be.

The last objection is one of timing and phasing. A quick answer is to refrain from hiring implementers until the specifications are complete. This is what is done when a building is constructed.

In the computer systems business, however, the pace is quicker, and one wants to compress the schedule as much as possible. How much can specification and building be overlapped?

As Blaauw points out, the total creative effort involves three distinct phases: architecture, implementation, and realization. It turns out that these can in fact be begun in parallel and proceed simultaneously.

In computer design, for example, the implementer can start as soon as he has relatively vague assumptions about the manual, somewhat clearer ideas about the technology, and well-defined cost and performance objectives. He can begin designing data flows, control sequences, gross packaging concepts, and so on. He devises or adapts the tools he will need, especially the record-keeping system, including the design automation system.

Meanwhile, at the realization level, circuits, cards, cables, frames, power supplies, and memories must each be designed, refined, and documented. This work proceeds in parallel with architecture and implementation.

The same thing is true in programming system design. Long before the external specifications are complete, the implementer has plenty to do. Given some rough approximations as to the function of the system that will be ultimately embodied in the external specifications, he can proceed. He must have well-defined space and time objectives. He must know the system configuration on which his product must run. Then he can begin designing module boundaries, table structures, pass or phase breakdowns, algorithms, and all kinds of tools. Some time, too, must be spent in communicating with the architect.

Meanwhile, on the realization level there is much to be done also. Programming has a technology, too. If the machine is a new one, much work must be done on subroutine conventions, supervisory techniques, searching and sorting algorithms.[7]

Conceptual integrity does require that a system reflect a single philosophy and that the specification as seen by the user flow from a few minds. Because of the real division of labor into architecture, implementation, and realization, however, this does not imply that a system so designed will take longer to build. Experience shows the opposite, that the integral system goes together faster and takes less time to test. In effect, a widespread horizontal division of labor has been sharply reduced by a vertical division of labor, and the result is radically simplified communications and improved conceptual integrity.

5
The Second-System Effect

5
The Second-System Effect

Adde parvum parvo magnus acervus erit.
[Add little to little and there will be a big pile.]

OVID

Turning house for air traffic. Lithograph, Paris, 1882
The Bettman Archive

If one separates responsibility for functional specification from responsibility for building a fast, cheap product, what discipline bounds the architect's inventive enthusiasm?

The fundamental answer is thoroughgoing, careful, and sympathetic communication between architect and builder. Nevertheless there are finer-grained answers that deserve attention.

Interactive Discipline for the Architect

The architect of a building works against a budget, using estimating techniques that are later confirmed or corrected by the contractors' bids. It often happens that all the bids exceed the budget. The architect then revises his estimating technique upward and his design downward for another iteration. He may perhaps suggest to the contractors ways to implement his design more cheaply than they had devised.

An analogous process governs the architect of a computer system or a programming system. He has, however, the advantage of getting bids from the contractor at many early points in his design, almost any time he asks for them. He usually has the disadvantage of working with only one contractor, who can raise or lower his estimates to reflect his pleasure with the design. In practice, early and continuous communication can give the architect good cost readings and the builder confidence in the design without blurring the clear division of responsibilities.

The architect has two possible answers when confronted with an estimate that is too high: cut the design or challenge the estimate by suggesting cheaper implementations. This latter is inherently an emotion-generating activity. The architect is now challenging the builder's way of doing the builder's job. For it to be successful, the architect must

- remember that the builder has the inventive and creative responsibility for the implementation; so the architect suggests, not dictates;

- always be prepared to suggest a way of implementing anything he specifies, and be prepared to accept any other way that meets the objectives as well;
- deal quietly and privately in such suggestions;
- be ready to forego credit for suggested improvements.

Normally the builder will counter by suggesting changes to the architecture. Often he is right—some minor feature may have unexpectedly large costs when the implementation is worked out.

Self-Discipline—The Second-System Effect

An architect's first work is apt to be spare and clean. He knows he doesn't know what he's doing, so he does it carefully and with great restraint.

As he designs the first work, frill after frill and embellishment after embellishment occur to him. These get stored away to be used "next time." Sooner or later the first system is finished, and the architect, with firm confidence and a demonstrated mastery of that class of systems, is ready to build a second system.

This second is the most dangerous system a man ever designs. When he does his third and later ones, his prior experiences will confirm each other as to the general characteristics of such systems, and their differences will identify those parts of his experience that are particular and not generalizable.

The general tendency is to over-design the second system, using all the ideas and frills that were cautiously sidetracked on the first one. The result, as Ovid says, is a "big pile." For example, consider the IBM 709 architecture, later embodied in the 7090. This is an upgrade, a second system for the very successful and clean 704. The operation set is so rich and profuse that only about half of it was regularly used.

Consider as a stronger case the architecture, implementation, and even the realization of the Stretch computer, an outlet for the pent-up inventive desires of many people, and a second system for most of them. As Strachey says in a review:

> *I get the impression that Stretch is in some way the end of one line of development. Like some early computer programs it is immensely ingenious, immensely complicated, and extremely effective, but somehow at the same time crude, wasteful, and inelegant, and one feels that there must be a better way of doing things.* [1]

Operating System/360 was the second system for most of its designers. Groups of its designers came from building the 1410-7010 disk operating system, the Stretch operating system, the Project Mercury real-time system, and IBSYS for the 7090. Hardly anyone had experience with *two* previous operating systems. [2] So OS/360 is a prime example of the second-system effect, a Stretch of the software art to which both the commendations and the reproaches of Strachey's critique apply unchanged.

For example, OS/360 devotes 26 bytes of the permanently resident date-turnover routine to the proper handling of December 31 on leap years (when it is Day 366). That might have been left to the operator.

The second-system effect has another manifestation somewhat different from pure functional embellishment. That is a tendency to refine techniques whose very existence has been made obsolete by changes in basic system assumptions. OS/360 has many examples of this.

Consider the linkage editor, designed to load separately-compiled programs and resolve their cross-references. Beyond this basic function it also handles program overlays. It is one of the finest overlay facilities ever built. It allows overlay structuring to be done externally, at linkage time, without being designed into the source code. It allows the overlay structure to be changed from run to run without recompilation. It furnishes a rich variety of useful options and facilities. In a sense it is the culmination of years of development of static overlay technique.

Yet it is also the last and finest of the dinosaurs, for it belongs to a system in which multiprogramming is the normal mode and dynamic core allocation the basic assumption. This is in direct conflict with the notion of using static overlays. How much better the system would work if the efforts devoted to overlay management had been spent on making the dynamic core allocation and the dynamic cross-referencing facilities really fast!

Furthermore, the linkage editor requires so much space and itself contains many overlays that even when it is used just for linkage without overlay management, it is slower than most of the system compilers. The irony of this is that the purpose of the linker is to avoid recompilation. Like a skater whose stomach gets ahead of his feet, refinement proceeded until the system assumptions had been quite outrun.

The TESTRAN debugging facility is another example of this tendency. It is the culmination of batch debugging facilities, furnishing truly elegant snapshot and core dump capabilities. It uses the control section concept and an ingenious generator technique to allow selective tracing and snapshotting without interpretive overhead or recompilation. The imaginative concepts of the Share Operating System[3] for the 709 have been brought to full bloom.

Meanwhile, the whole notion of batch debugging without recompilation was becoming obsolete. Interactive computing systems, using language interpreters or incremental compilers have provided the most fundamental challenge. But even in batch systems, the appearance of fast-compile/slow-execute compilers has made source-level debugging and snapshotting the preferred technique. How much better the system would have been if the TESTRAN effort had been devoted instead to building the interactive and fast-compile facilities earlier and better!

Yet another example is the scheduler, which provides truly excellent facilities for managing a fixed-batch job stream. In a real sense, this scheduler is the refined, improved, and embellished second system succeeding the 1410-7010 Disk Operating System, a batch system unmultiprogrammed except for input-output and intended chiefly for business applications. As such, the OS/360 scheduler is good. But it is almost totally uninfluenced by the OS/360 needs of remote job entry, multiprogramming, and permanently resident interactive subsystems. Indeed, the scheduler's design makes these hard.

How does the architect avoid the second-system effect? Well, obviously he can't skip his second system. But he can be conscious of the peculiar hazards of that system, and exert extra self-discipline to avoid functional ornamentation and to avoid extrapolation of functions that are obviated by changes in assumptions and purposes.

A discipline that will open an architect's eyes is to assign each little function a value: capability x is worth not more than m bytes of memory and n microseconds per invocation. These values will guide initial decisions and serve during implementation as a guide and warning to all.

How does the project manager avoid the second-system effect? By insisting on a senior architect who has at least two systems under his belt. Too, by staying aware of the special temptations, he can ask the right questions to ensure that the philosophical concepts and objectives are fully reflected in the detailed design.

6
Passing the Word

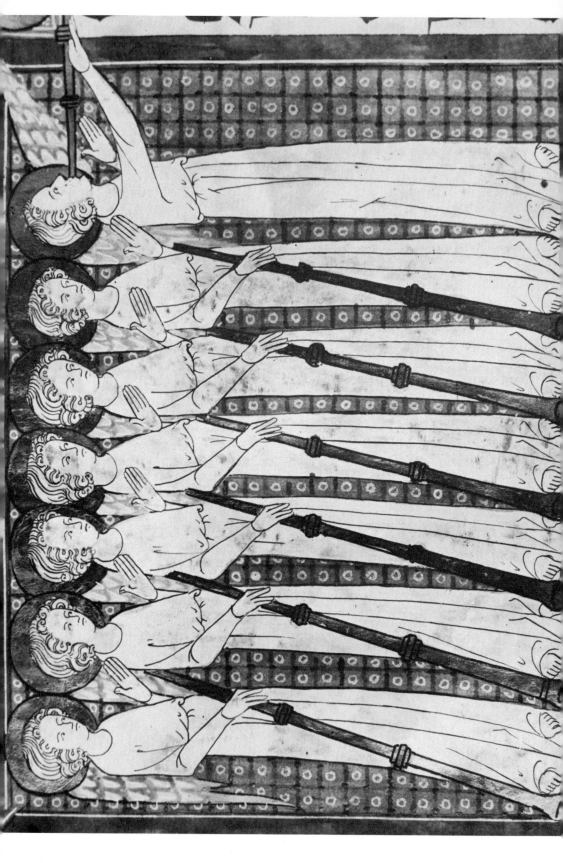

6
Passing the Word

He'll sit here and he'll say, "Do this! Do that!" And nothing will happen.

HARRY S. TRUMAN, ON PRESIDENTIAL POWER [1]

"The Seven Trumpets" from *The Wells Apocalypse,* 14th century
The Bettman Archive

Assuming that he has the disciplined, experienced architects and that there are many implementers, how shall the manager ensure that everyone hears, understands, and implements the architects' decisions? How can a group of 10 architects maintain the conceptual integrity of a system which 1000 men are building? A whole technology for doing this was worked out for the System/360 hardware design effort, and it is equally applicable to software projects.

Written Specifications—the Manual

The manual, or written specification, is a necessary tool, though not a sufficient one. The manual is the *external* specification of the product. It describes and prescribes every detail of what the user sees. As such, it is the chief product of the architect.

Round and round goes its preparation cycle, as feedback from users and implementers shows where the design is awkward to use or build. For the sake of implementers it is important that the changes be quantized—that there be dated versions appearing on a schedule.

The manual must not only describe everything the user does see, including all interfaces; it must also refrain from describing what the user does not see. That is the implementer's business, and there his design freedom must be unconstrained. The architect must always be prepared to show *an* implementation for any feature he describes, but he must not attempt to dictate *the* implementation.

The style must be precise, full, and accurately detailed. A user will often refer to a single definition, so each one must repeat all the essentials and yet all must agree. This tends to make manuals dull reading, but precision is more important than liveliness.

The unity of System/360's *Principles of Operation* springs from the fact that only two pens wrote it: Gerry Blaauw's and Andris Padegs'. The ideas are those of about ten men, but the casting of those decisions into prose specifications must be done by only one or two, if the consistency of prose and product is to be maintained. For the writing of a definition will necessitate a host of mini-decisions which are not of full-debate importance. An example in System/360 is the detail of how the Condition Code is set after each operation. *Not* trivial, however, is the principle that such mini-decisions be made consistently throughout.

I think the finest piece of manual writing I have ever seen is Blaauw's Appendix to *System/360 Principles of Operation.* This describes with care and precision the *limits* of System/360 compatibility. It defines compatibility, prescribes what is to be achieved, and enumerates those areas of external appearance where the architecture is intentionally silent and where results from one model may differ from those of another, where one copy of a given model may differ from another copy, or where a copy may differ even from itself after an engineering change. This is the level of precision to which manual writers aspire, and they must define what is *not* prescribed as carefully as what is.

Formal Definitions

English, or any other human language, is not naturally a precision instrument for such definitions. Therefore the manual writer must strain himself and his language to achieve the precision needed. An attractive alternative is to use a formal notation for such definitions. After all, precision is the stock in trade, the *raison d'être* of formal notations.

Let us examine the merits and weaknesses of formal definitions. As noted, formal definitions are precise. They tend to be complete; gaps show more conspicuously, so they are filled sooner. What they lack is comprehensibility. With English prose one can show structural principles, delineate structure in stages or levels, and give examples. One can readily mark exceptions and emphasize contrasts. Most important, one can explain *why.* The formal definitions put forward so far have inspired wonder at their elegance and confidence in their precision. But they have demanded prose explanations to make their content easy to learn and teach. For these reasons, I think we will see future specifications to consist of both a formal definition *and* a prose definition.

An ancient adage warns, "Never go to sea with two chronometers; take one or three." The same thing clearly applies to prose and formal definitions. If one has both, one must be the standard, and the other must be a derivative description, clearly labeled as such. Either can be the primary standard. Algol 68 has a formal definition as standard and a prose definition as descriptive. PL/I has the prose as standard and the formal description as derivative. System/360 also has prose as standard with a derived formal description.

Many tools are available for formal definition. The Backus-Naur Form is familiar for language definition, and it is amply discussed in the literature.[2] The formal description of PL/I uses new notions of abstract syntax, and it is adequately described.[3] Iverson's APL has been used to describe machines, most notably the IBM 7090[4] and System/360.[5]

Bell and Newell have proposed new notations for describing both configurations and machine architectures, and they have illustrated these with several machines, including the DEC PDP-8,[6] the 7090,[6] and System/360.[7]

Almost all formal definitions turn out to embody or describe an implementation of the hardware or software system whose externals they are prescribing. Syntax can be described without this, but semantics are usually defined by giving a program that carries out the defined operation. This is of course an implementation, and as such it over-prescribes the architecture. So one must take care to indicate that the formal definition applies only to externals, and one must say what these are.

Not only is a formal definition an implementation, an implementation can serve as a formal definition. When the first compatible computers were built, this was exactly the technique used. The new machine was to match an existing machine. The manual was vague on some points? "Ask the machine!" A test program would be devised to determine the behavior, and the new machine would be built to match.

A programmed simulator of a hardware or software system can serve in precisely the same way. It is an implementation; it runs. So all questions of definition can be resolved by testing it.

Using an implementation as a definition has some advantages. All questions can be settled unambiguously by experiment. Debate is never needed, so answers are quick. Answers are always as precise as one wants, and they are always correct, by definition. Opposed to these one has a formidable set of disadvantages. The implementation may over-prescribe even the externals. Invalid syntax always produces some result; in a policed system that result is an invalidity indication *and nothing more.* In an unpoliced system all kinds of side effects may appear, and these may have been used by programmers. When we undertook to emulate the IBM 1401 on System/360, for example, it developed that there were 30 different "curios"—side effects of supposedly invalid operations— that had come into widespread use and had to be considered as part of the definition. The implementation as a definition overprescribed; it not only said what the machine must do, it also said a great deal about how it had to do it.

Then, too, the implementation will sometimes give unexpected and unplanned answers when sharp questions are asked, and the *de facto* definition will often be found to be inelegant in these particulars precisely because they have never received any thought. This inelegance will often turn out to be slow or costly to duplicate in another implementation. For example, some machines leave trash in the multiplicand register after a multiplication. The precise nature of this trash turns out to be part of the *de facto* definition, yet duplicating it may preclude the use of a faster multiplication algorithm.

Finally, the use of an implementation as a formal definition is peculiarly susceptible to confusion as to whether the prose description or the formal description is in fact the standard. This is especially true of programmed simulations. One must also refrain from modifications to the implementation while it is serving as a standard.

Direct Incorporation

A lovely technique for disseminating and enforcing definitions is available for the software system architect. It is especially useful for establishing the syntax, if not the semantics, of intermodule interfaces. This technique is to design the declaration of the passed parameters or shared storage, and to require the implementations to include that declaration via a compile-time operation (a macro or a %INCLUDE in PL/I). If, in addition, the whole interface is referenced only by symbolic names, the declaration can be changed by adding or inserting new variables with only recompilation, not alteration, of the using program.

Conferences and Courts

Needless to say, meetings are necessary. The hundreds of man-to-man consultations must be supplemented by larger and more formal gatherings. We found two levels of these to be useful. The first is a weekly half-day conference of all the architects, plus official representatives of the hardware and software implementers, and the market planners. The chief system architect presides.

Anyone can propose problems or changes, but proposals are usually distributed in writing before the meeting. A new problem is usually discussed a while. The emphasis is on creativity, rather than merely decision. The group attempts to invent many solutions to problems, then a few solutions are passed to one or more of the architects for detailing into precisely worded manual change proposals.

Detailed change proposals then come up for decisions. These have been circulated and carefully considered by implementers and users, and the pros and cons are well delineated. If a consensus emerges, well and good. If not, the chief architect decides. Minutes are kept and decisions are formally, promptly, and widely disseminated.

Decisions from the weekly conferences give quick results and allow work to proceed. If anyone is *too* unhappy, instant appeals to the project manager are possible, but this happens very rarely.

The fruitfulness of these meetings springs from several sources:

1. The same group—architects, users, and implementers—meets weekly for months. No time is needed for bringing people up to date.
2. The group is bright, resourceful, well versed in the issues, and deeply involved in the outcome. No one has an "advisory" role. Everyone is authorized to make binding commitments.
3. When problems are raised, solutions are sought both within and outside the obvious boundaries.
4. The formality of written proposals focuses attention, forces decision, and avoids committee-drafted inconsistencies.
5. The clear vesting of decision-making power in the chief architect avoids compromise and delay.

As time goes by, some decisions don't wear well. Some minor matters have never been wholeheartedly accepted by one or another of the participants. Other decisions have developed unforeseen problems, and sometimes the weekly meeting didn't agree to reconsider these. So there builds up a backlog of minor appeals, open issues, or disgruntlements. To settle these we held annual supreme court sessions, lasting typically two weeks. (I would hold them every six months if I were doing it again.)

These sessions were held just before major freeze dates for the manual. Those present included not only the architecture group and the programmers' and implementers' architectural representatives, but also the managers of programming, marketing, and implementation efforts. The System/360 project manager presided. The agenda typically consisted of about 200 items, mostly minor, which were enumerated in charts placarded around the room. All sides were heard and decisions made. By the miracle of computer-ized text editing (and lots of fine staff work), each participant found an updated manual, embodying yesterday's decisions, at his seat every morning.

These "fall festivals" were useful not only for resolving deci-sions, but also for getting them accepted. Everyone was heard, everyone participated, everyone understood better the intricate constraints and interrelationships among decisions.

Multiple Implementations

System/360 architects had two almost unprecedented advantages: enough time to work carefully, and political clout equal to that of the implementers. The provision of enough time came from the schedule of the new technology; the political equality came from the simultaneous construction of multiple implementations. The necessity for strict compatibility among these served as the best possible enforcing agent for the specifications.

In most computer projects there comes a day when it is discov-ered that the machine and the manual don't agree. When the confrontation follows, the manual usually loses, for it can be changed far more quickly and cheaply than the machine. Not so, however, when there are multiple implementations. Then the de-lays and costs associated with fixing the errant machine can be overmatched by delays and costs in revising the machines that followed the manual faithfully.

This notion can be fruitfully applied whenever a programming language is being defined. One can be certain that several inter-preters or compilers will sooner or later have to be built to meet various objectives. The definition will be cleaner and the discipline tighter if at least two implementations are built initially.

The Telephone Log

As implementation proceeds, countless questions of architectural interpretation arise, no matter how precise the specification. Obviously many such questions require amplifications and clarifications in the text. Others merely reflect misunderstandings.

It is essential, however, to encourage the puzzled implementer to telephone the responsible architect and ask his question, rather than to guess and proceed. It is just as vital to recognize that the answers to such questions are *ex cathedra* architectural pronouncements that must be told to everyone.

One useful mechanism is a *telephone log* kept by the architect. In it he records every question and every answer. Each week the logs of the several architects are concatenated, reproduced, and distributed to the users and implementers. While this mechanism is quite informal, it is both quick and comprehensive.

Product Test

The project manager's best friend is his daily adversary, the independent product-testing organization. This group checks machines and programs against specifications and serves as a devil's advocate, pinpointing every conceivable defect and discrepancy. Every development organization needs such an independent technical auditing group to keep it honest.

In the last analysis the customer is the independent auditor. In the merciless light of real use, every flaw will show. The product-testing group then is the surrogate customer, specialized for finding flaws. Time after time, the careful product tester will find places where the word didn't get passed, where the design decisions were not properly understood or accurately implemented. For this reason such a testing group is a necessary link in the chain by which the design word is passed, a link that needs to operate early and simultaneously with design.

7
Why Did the Tower of Babel Fail?

7
Why Did the Tower of Babel Fail?

Now the whole earth used only one language, with few words. On the occasion of a migration from the east, men discovered a plain in the land of Shinar, and settled there. Then they said to one another, "Come, let us make bricks, burning them well." So they used bricks for stone, and bitumen for mortar. Then they said, "Come, let us build ourselves a city with a tower whose top shall reach the heavens (thus making a name for ourselves), so that we may not be scattered all over the earth." Then the Lord came down to look at the city and tower which human beings had built. The Lord said, "They are just one people, and they all have the same language. If this is what they can do as a beginning, then nothing that they resolve to do will be impossible for them. Come, let us go down, and there make such a babble of their language that they will not understand one another's speech." Thus the Lord dispersed them from there all over the earth, so that they had to stop building the city.

GENESIS 11:1–8

P. Breughel, the Elder, "Turmbau zu Babel," 1563
Kunsthistorisches Museum, Vienna

A Management Audit of the Babel Project

According to the Genesis account, the tower of Babel was man's second major engineering undertaking, after Noah's ark. Babel was the first engineering fiasco.

The story is deep and instructive on several levels. Let us, however, examine it purely as an engineering project, and see what management lessons can be learned. How well was their project equipped with the prerequisites for success? Did they have:

1. A *clear mission?* Yes, although naively impossible. The project failed long before it ran into this fundamental limitation.
2. *Manpower?* Plenty of it.
3. *Materials?* Clay and asphalt are abundant in Mesopotamia.
4. Enough *time?* Yes, there is no hint of any time constraint.
5. Adequate *technology?* Yes, the pyramidal or conical structure is inherently stable and spreads the compressive load well. Clearly masonry was well understood. The project failed before it hit technological limitations.

Well, if they had all of these things, why did the project fail? Where did they lack? In two respects—*communication,* and its consequent, *organization.* They were unable to talk with each other; hence they could not coordinate. When coordination failed, work ground to a halt. Reading between the lines we gather that lack of communication led to disputes, bad feelings, and group jealousies. Shortly the clans began to move apart, preferring isolation to wrangling.

Communication in the Large Programming Project

So it is today. Schedule disaster, functional misfits, and system bugs all arise because the left hand doesn't know what the right hand is doing. As work proceeds, the several teams slowly change the functions, sizes, and speeds of their own programs, and they explicitly or implicitly change their assumptions about the inputs available and the uses to be made of the outputs.

For example, the implementer of a program-overlaying function may run into problems and reduce speed, relying on statistics that show how rarely this function will arise in application programs. Meanwhile, back at the ranch, his neighbor may be designing a major part of the supervisor so that it critically depends upon the speed of this function. This change in speed itself becomes a major specification change, and it needs to be proclaimed abroad and weighed from a system point of view.

How, then, shall teams communicate with one another? In as many ways as possible.

- *Informally.* Good telephone service and a clear definition of intergroup dependencies will encourage the hundreds of calls upon which common interpretation of written documents depends.
- *Meetings.* Regular project meetings, with one team after another giving technical briefings, are invaluable. Hundreds of minor misunderstandings get smoked out this way.
- *Workbook.* A formal project workbook must be started at the beginning. This deserves a section by itself.

The Project Workbook

What. The project workbook is not so much a separate document as it is a structure imposed on the documents that the project will be producing anyway.

All the documents of the project need to be part of this structure. This includes objectives, external specifications, interface specifications, technical standards, internal specifications, and administrative memoranda.

Why. Technical prose is almost immortal. If one examines the genealogy of a customer manual for a piece of hardware or software, one can trace not only the ideas, but also many of the very sentences and paragraphs back to the first memoranda proposing the product or explaining the first design. For the technical writer, the paste-pot is as mighty as the pen.

Since this is so, and since tomorrow's product-quality manuals will grow from today's memos, it is very important to get the structure of the documentation right. The early design of the project workbook ensures that the documentation structure itself is crafted, not haphazard. Moreover, the establishment of a structure molds later writing into segments that fit into that structure.

The second reason for the project workbook is control of the distribution of information. The problem is not to restrict information, but to ensure that relevant information gets to all the people who need it.

The first step is to number all memoranda, so that ordered lists of titles are available and each worker can see if he has what he wants. The organization of the workbook goes well beyond this to establish a tree-structure of memoranda. The tree-structure allows distribution lists to be maintained by subtree, if that is desirable.

Mechanics.   As with so many programming management problems, the technical memorandum problem gets worse nonlinearly as size increases. With 10 people, documents can simply be numbered. With 100 people, several linear sequences will often suffice. With 1000, scattered inevitably over several physical locations, the *need* for a structured workbook increases and the *size* of the workbook increases. How then shall the mechanics be handled?

I think this was well done on the OS/360 project. The need for a well-structured workbook was strongly urged by O. S. Locken, who had seen its effectiveness on his previous project, the 1410-7010 operating system.

We quickly decided that *each* programmer should see *all* the material, i.e., should have a copy of the workbook in his own office.

Of critical importance is timely updating. The workbook must be current. This is very difficult to do if whole documents must be retyped for changes. In a looseleaf book, however, only pages need to be changed. We had available a computer-driven text-editing system, and this proved invaluable for timely maintenance. Offset masters were prepared directly on the computer printer, and turnaround time was less than a day. The recipient of all these updated pages has an assimilation problem, however. When he first receives a changed page, he wants to know, "What has been changed?" When he later consults it, he wants to know, "What is the definition today?"

The latter need is met by the continually maintained document. Highlighting of changes requires other steps. First, one must mark changed text on the page, e.g., by a vertical bar in the margin alongside every altered line. Second, one needs to distribute with the new pages a short, separately written change summary that lists the changes and remarks on their significance.

Our project had not been under way six months before we hit another problem. The workbook was about five feet thick! If we had stacked up the 100 copies serving programmers in our offices in Manhattan's Time-Life Building, they would have towered above the building itself. Furthermore, the daily change distribution averaged two inches, some 150 pages to be interfiled in the whole. Maintenance of the workbook began to take a significant time from each workday.

At this point we switched to microfiche, a change that saved a million dollars, even allowing for the cost of a microfiche reader for each office. We were able to arrange excellent turnaround on microfiche production; the workbook shrank from three cubic feet to one-sixth of a cubic foot and, most significantly, updates appeared in hundred-page chunks, reducing the interfiling problem a hundredfold.

Microfiche has its drawbacks. From the manager's point of view the awkward interfiling of paper pages ensured that the changes were *read,* which was the purpose of the workbook. Microfiche would make workbook maintenance too easy, unless the update fiche are distributed with a paper document enumerating the changes.

Also, a microfiche cannot readily be highlighted, marked, and commented by the reader. Documents with which the reader has interacted are more effective for the author and more useful for the reader.

On balance I think the microfiche was a very happy mechanism, and I would recommend it over a paper workbook for very large projects.

How would one do it today? With today's system technology available, I think the technique of choice is to keep the workbook on the direct-access file, marked with change bars and revision dates. Each user would consult it from a display terminal (typewriters are too slow). A change summary, prepared daily, would be stored in LIFO fashion at a fixed access point. The programmer would probably read that daily, but if he missed a day he would need only read longer the next day. As he read the change summary, he could interrupt to consult the changed text itself.

Notice that the workbook itself is not changed. It is still the assemblage of all project documentation, structured according to a careful design. The only change is in the mechanics of distribution and consultation. D. C. Engelbart and his colleagues at the Stanford Research Institute have built such a system and are using it to build and maintain documentation for the ARPA network.

D. L. Parnas of Carnegie-Mellon University has proposed a still more radical solution.[1] His thesis is that the programmer is most effective if shielded from, rather than exposed to the details of construction of system parts other than his own. This presupposes that all interfaces are completely and precisely defined. While that is definitely sound design, dependence upon its perfect accomplishment is a recipe for disaster. A good information system both exposes interface errors and stimulates their correction.

Organization in the Large Programming Project

If there are n workers on a project, there are $(n^2-n)/2$ interfaces across which there may be communication, and there are potentially almost 2^n teams within which coordination must occur. The purpose of organization is to reduce the amount of communication and coordination necessary; hence organization is a radical attack on the communication problems treated above.

The means by which communication is obviated are *division of labor* and *specialization of function.* The tree-like structure of organizations reflects the diminishing need for detailed communication when division and specialization of labor are applied.

In fact, a tree organization really arises as a structure of authority and responsibility. The principle that no man can serve two masters dictates that the authority structure be tree-like. But the communication structure is not so restricted, and the tree is a barely passable approximation to the communication structure, which is a network. The inadequacies of the tree approximation give rise to staff groups, task forces, committees, and even the matrix-type organization used in many engineering laboratories.

Let us consider a tree-like programming organization, and examine the essentials which any subtree must have in order to be effective. They are:

1. a mission
2. a producer
3. a technical director or architect
4. a schedule
5. a division of labor
6. interface definitions among the parts

All of this is obvious and conventional except the distinction between the producer and the technical director. Let us first consider the two roles, then their relationship.

What is the role of the producer? He assembles the team, divides the work, and establishes the schedule. He acquires and keeps on acquiring the necessary resources. This means that a major part of his role is communication outside the team, upwards and sideways. He establishes the pattern of communication and reporting within the team. Finally, he ensures that the schedule is met, shifting resources and organization to respond to changing circumstances.

How about the technical director? He conceives of the design to be built, identifies its subparts, specifies how it will look from outside, and sketches its internal structure. He provides unity and conceptual integrity to the whole design; thus he serves as a limit on system complexity. As individual technical problems arise, he invents solutions for them or shifts the system design as required. He is, in Al Capp's lovely phrase, "inside-man at the skunk works." His communications are chiefly within the team. His work is almost completely technical.

Now it is clear that the talents required for these two roles are quite different. Talents come in many different combinations; and the particular combination embodied in the producer and the director must govern the relationship between them. Organizations must be designed around the people available; not people fitted into pure-theory organizations.

Three relationships are possible, and all three are found in successful practice.

The producer and the technical director may be the same man. This is readily workable on very small teams, perhaps three to six programmers. On larger projects it is very rarely workable, for two reasons. First, the man with strong management talent and strong technical talent is rarely found. Thinkers are rare; doers are rarer; and thinker-doers are rarest.

Second, on the larger project each of the roles is necessarily a full-time job, or more. It is hard for the producer to delegate enough of his duties to give him any technical time. It is impossible for the director to delegate his without compromising the conceptual integrity of the design.

The producer may be boss, the director his right-hand man. The difficulty here is to establish the director's *authority* to make technical decisions without impacting his time as would putting him in the management chain-of-command.

Obviously the producer must proclaim the director's technical authority, and he must back it in an extremely high proportion of the test cases that will arise. For this to be possible, the producer and the director must see alike on fundamental technical philosophy; they must talk out the main technical issues privately, before they really become timely; and the producer must have a high respect for the director's technical prowess.

Less obviously, the producer can do all sorts of subtle things with the symbols of status (office size, carpet, furnishing, carbon copies, etc.) to proclaim that the director, although outside the management line, is a source of decision power.

This can be made to work very effectively. Unfortunately it is rarely tried. The job done least well by project managers is to utilize the technical genius who is not strong on management talent.

The director may be boss, and the producer his right-hand man. Robert Heinlein, in *The Man Who Sold the Moon*, describes such an arrangement in a graphic for-instance:

> *Coster buried his face in his hands, then looked up. "I know it. I know what needs to be done—but every time I try to tackle a technical problem some bloody fool wants me to make a decision about trucks —or telephones—or some damn thing. I'm sorry, Mr. Harriman. I thought I could do it."*
>
> *Harriman said very gently, "Don't let it throw you, Bob. You haven't had much sleep lately, have you? Tell you what—we'll put over a fast one on Ferguson. I'll take that desk you're at for a few days and build you a set-up to protect you against such things. I want that brain of yours thinking about reaction vectors and fuel efficiencies and design stresses, not about contracts for trucks." Harriman stepped to the door, looked around the outer office and spotted a man who might or might not be the office's chief clerk. "Hey you! C'mere."*
>
> *The man looked startled, got up, came to the door and said, "Yes?"*
>
> *"I want that desk in the corner and all the stuff that's on it moved to an empty office on this floor, right away."*

He supervised getting Coster and his other desk moved into another office, saw to it that the phone in the new office was disconnected, and, as an afterthought, had a couch moved in there, too. "We'll install a projector, and a drafting machine and bookcases and other junk like that tonight," he told Coster. "Just make a list of anything you need —to work on engineering." *He went back to the nominal chief-engineer's office and got happily to work trying to figure where the organization stood and what was wrong with it.*

Some four hours later he took Berkeley in to meet Coster. The chief engineer was asleep at his desk, head cradled on his arms. Harriman started to back out, but Coster roused. "Oh! Sorry," he said, blushing, "I must have dozed off."

"That's why I brought you the couch," said Harriman. "It's more restful. Bob, meet Jock Berkeley. He's your new slave. You remain chief engineer and top, undisputed boss. Jock is Lord High Everything Else. From now on you've got absolutely nothing to worry about— except for the little detail of building a Moon ship."

They shook hands. "Just one thing I ask, Mr. Coster," Berkeley said seriously, "bypass me all you want to—you'll have to run the technical show—but for God's sake record it so I'll know what's going on. I'm going to have a switch placed on your desk that will operate a sealed recorder at my desk."

"Fine!" Coster was looking, Harriman thought, younger already.

"And if you want something that is not technical, don't do it yourself. Just flip a switch and whistle; it'll get done!" Berkeley glanced at Harriman. "The Boss says he wants to talk with you about the real job. I'll leave you and get busy." He left.

Harriman sat down; Coster followed suit and said, "Whew!"

"Feel better?"

"I like the looks of that fellow Berkeley."

"That's good; he's your twin brother from now on. Stop worrying; I've used him before. You'll think you're living in a well-run hospital."[2]

This account hardly needs any analytic commentary. This arrangement, too, can be made to work effectively.

I suspect that the last arrangement is best for small teams, as discussed in Chapter 3, "The Surgical Team." I think the producer as boss is a more suitable arrangement for the larger subtrees of a really big project.

The Tower of Babel was perhaps the first engineering fiasco, but it was not the last. Communication and its consequent, organization, are critical for success. The techniques of communication and organization demand from the manager much thought and as much experienced competence as the software technology itself.

8
Calling the Shot

8
Calling the Shot

Practice is the best of all instructors.

PUBLILIUS

Experience is a dear teacher, but fools will learn at no other.

POOR RICHARD'S ALMANAC

Douglass Crockwell, "Ruth calls his shot," World Series, 1932
Reproduced by permission of Esquire Magazine and Douglass Crockwell, © 1945 (renewed 1973) by Esquire, Inc., and courtesy of the National Baseball Museum.

How long will a system programming job take? How much effort will be required? How does one estimate?

I have earlier suggested ratios that seem to apply to planning time, coding, component test, and system test. First, one must say that one does *not* estimate the entire task by estimating the coding portion only and then applying the ratios. The coding is only one-sixth or so of the problem, and errors in its estimate or in the ratios could lead to ridiculous results.

Second, one must say that data for building isolated small programs are not applicable to programming systems products. For a program averaging about 3200 words, for example, Sackman, Erikson, and Grant report an average code-plus-debug time of about 178 hours for a single programmer, a figure which would extrapolate to give an annual productivity of 35,800 statements per year. A program half that size took less than one-fourth as long, and extrapolated productivity is almost 80,000 statements per year.[1] Planning, documentation, testing, system integration, and training times must be added. The linear extrapolation of such sprint figures is meaningless. Extrapolation of times for the hundred-yard dash shows that a man can run a mile in under three minutes.

Before dismissing them, however, let us note that these numbers, although not for strictly comparable problems, suggest that effort goes as a power of size *even* when no communication is involved except that of a man with his memories.

Figure 8.1 tells the sad story. It illustrates results reported from a study done by Nanus and Farr[2] at System Development Corporation. This shows an exponent of 1.5; that is,

$$\text{effort} = (\text{constant}) \times (\text{number of instructions})^{1.5}.$$

Another SDC study reported by Weinwurm[3] also shows an exponent near 1.5.

A few studies on programmer productivity have been made, and several estimating techniques have been proposed. Morin has prepared a survey of the published data.[4] Here I shall give only a few items that seem especially illuminating.

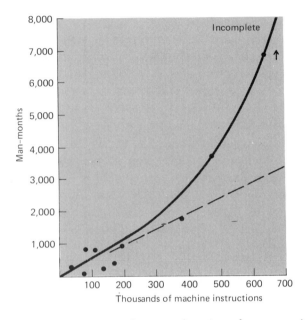

Fig. 8.1   Programming effort as a function of program size

Portman's Data

Charles Portman, manager of ICL's Software Division, Computer Equipment Organization (Northwest) at Manchester, offers another useful personal insight.[5]

He found his programming teams missing schedules by about one-half—each job was taking approximately twice as long as estimated. The estimates were very careful, done by experienced teams estimating man-hours for several hundred subtasks on a PERT chart. When the slippage pattern appeared, he asked them to keep careful daily logs of time usage. These showed that the estimating error could be entirely accounted for by the fact that his teams were only realizing 50 percent of the working week as actual programming and debugging time. Machine downtime, higher-priority short unrelated jobs, meetings, paperwork, company business, sickness, personal time, etc. accounted for the rest. In short, the estimates made an unrealistic assumption about the number of technical work hours per man-year. My own experience quite confirms his conclusion.[6]

Aron's Data

Joel Aron, manager of Systems Technology at IBM in Gaithersburg, Maryland, has studied programmer productivity when working on nine large systems (briefly, *large* means more than 25 programmers and 30,000 deliverable instructions).[7] He divides such systems according to interactions among programmers (and system parts) and finds productivities as follows:

Very few interactions   10,000 instructions per man-year
Some interactions   5,000
Many interactions   1,500

The man-years do not include support and system test activities, only design and programming. When these figures are diluted by a factor of two to cover system test, they closely match Harr's data.

Harr's Data

John Harr, manager of programming for the Bell Telephone Laboratories' Electronic Switching System, reported his and others' experience in a paper at the 1969 Spring Joint Computer Conference.[8] These data are shown in Figs. 8.2, 8.3, and 8.4.

Of these, Fig. 8.2 is the most detailed and the most useful. The first two jobs are basically control programs; the second two are basically language translators. Productivity is stated in terms of debugged words per man-year. This includes programming, component test, and system test. It is not clear how much of the planning effort, or effort in machine support, writing, and the like, is included.

	Prog. units	Number of programmers	Years	Man-years	Program words	Words/ man-yr.
Operational	50	83	4	101	52,000	515
Maintenance	36	60	4	81	51,000	630
Compiler	13	9	2¼	17	38,000	2230
Translator (Data assembler)	15	13	2½	11	25,000	2270

Fig. 8.2   Summary of four No. 1 ESS program jobs

The productivities likewise fall into two classifications; those for control programs are about 600 words per man-year; those for translators are about 2200 words per man-year. Note that all four programs are of similar size—the variation is in size of the work groups, length of time, and number of modules. Which is cause and which is effect? Did the control programs require more people because they were more complicated? Or did they require more modules and more man-months because they were assigned more people? Did they take longer because of the greater complexity, or because more people were assigned? One can't be sure. The control programs were surely more complex. These uncertainties aside, the numbers describe the real productivities achieved on a large system, using present-day programming techniques. As such they are a real contribution.

Figures 8.3 and 8.4 show some interesting data on programming and debugging rates as compared to predicted rates.

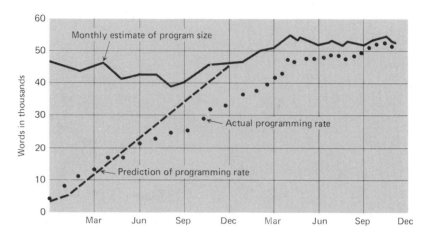

Fig. 8.3   ESS predicted and actual programming rates

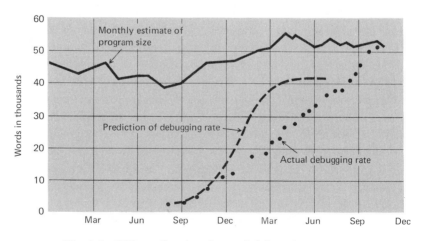

Fig. 8.4   ESS predicted and actual debugging rates

OS/360 Data

IBM OS/360 experience, while not available in the detail of Harr's data, confirms it. Productivities in range of 600–800 debugged instructions per man-year were experienced by control program groups. Productivities in the 2000–3000 debugged instructions per man-year were achieved by language translator groups. These include planning done by the group, coding component test, system test, and some support activities. They are comparable to Harr's data, so far as I can tell.

Aron's data, Harr's data, and the OS/360 data all confirm striking differences in productivity related to the complexity and difficulty of the task itself. My guideline in the morass of estimating complexity is that compilers are three times as bad as normal batch application programs, and operating systems are three times as bad as compilers.[9]

Corbató's Data

Both Harr's data and OS/360 data are for assembly language programming. Little data seem to have been published on system programming productivity using higher-level languages. Corbató of MIT's Project MAC reports, however, a mean productivity of 1200 lines of debugged PL/I statements per man-year on the MULTICS system (between 1 and 2 million words).[10]

This number is very exciting. Like the other projects, MULTICS includes control programs and language translators. Like the others, it is producing a system programming product, tested and documented. The data seem to be comparable in terms of kind of effort included. And the productivity number is a good average between the control program and translator productivities of other projects.

But Corbató's number is *lines* per man-year, not *words*! Each statement in his system corresponds to about three to five words of handwritten code! This suggests two important conclusions.

- Productivity seems constant in terms of elementary statements, a conclusion that is reasonable in terms of the thought a statement requires and the errors it may include.[11]
- Programming productivity may be increased as much as five times when a suitable high-level language is used.[12]

9

Ten Pounds
in a Five-Pound Sack

9
Ten Pounds
in a Five-Pound Sack

*The author should gaze at Noah, and . . . learn, as they
did in the Ark, to crowd a great deal of matter into a very
small compass.*

SYDNEY SMITH, EDINBURGH REVIEW

Engraved from a painting by Heywood Hardy
The Bettman Archive

Program Space as Cost

How big is it? Aside from running time, the space occupied by a program is a principal cost. This is true even for proprietary programs, where the user pays the author a fee that is essentially a share of the development cost. Consider the IBM APL interactive software system. It rents for $400 per month and, when used, takes at least 160 K bytes of memory. On a Model 165, memory rents for about $12 per kilobyte per month. If the program is available full-time, one pays $400 software rent and $1920 memory rent for using the program. If one uses the APL system only four hours a day, the costs are $400 software rent and $320 memory rent per month.

One frequently hears horror expressed that a 2 M byte machine may have 400 K devoted to its operating system. This is as foolish as criticizing a Boeing 747 because it costs $27 million. One must also ask, "What does it do?" What does one get in ease-of-use and in performance (via efficient system utilization) for the dollars so spent? Could the $4800 per month thus invested in memory rental have been more fruitfully spent for other hardware, for programmers, for application programs?

The system designer puts part of his total hardware resource into resident-program memory when he thinks it will do more for the user in that form than as adders, disks, etc. To do otherwise would be grossly irresponsible. And the result must be judged as a whole. No one can criticize a programming system for size *per se* and at the same time consistently advocate closer integration of hardware and software design.

Since size is such a large part of the user cost of a programming system product, the builder must set size targets, control size, and devise size-reduction techniques, just as the hardware builder sets component-count targets, controls component count, and devises count-reduction techniques. Like any cost, size itself is not bad, but unnecessary size is.

Size Control

For the project manager, size control is partly a technical job and partly a managerial one. One has to study users and their applications to set the sizes of the systems to be offered. Then these systems have to be subdivided, and each component given a size target. Since size-speed trade-offs come in rather big quantum jumps, setting size targets is a tricky business, requiring knowledge of the available trade-offs within each piece. The wise manager also saves himself a kitty, to be allocated as work proceeds.

In OS/360, even though all of this was done very carefully, still other lessons had to be painfully learned.

First, setting size targets for core is not enough; one has to budget all aspects of size. In most previous operating systems, systems residence had been on tape, and the long search times of tape meant that one was not tempted to use it casually to bring in program segments. OS/360 was disk-resident, like its immediate predecessors, the Stretch Operating System and the 1410-7010 Disk Operating System. Its builders rejoiced in the freedom of cheap disk accesses. The initial result was disastrous to performance.

In setting core sizes for each component, we had not simultaneously set access budgets. As anyone with 20-20 hindsight would expect, a programmer who found his program slopping over his core target broke it into overlays. This process in itself added to the total size and slowed execution down. Most seriously, our management control system neither measured nor caught this. Each man reported as to how much *core* he was using, and since he was within target, no one worried.

Fortunately, there came a day early in the effort when the OS/360 performance simulator began to work. The first result indicated deep trouble. Fortran H, on a Model 65 with drums, simulated compiling at five statements per minute! Digging-in showed that the control program modules were each making many, many disk accesses. Even high-frequency supervisor modules were making many trips to the well, and the result was quite analogous to page thrashing.

The first moral is clear: Set *total* size budgets as well as resident-space budgets; set budgets on backing-store accesses as well as on sizes.

The next lesson was very similar. The space budgets were set before precise functional allocations were made to each module. As a result, any programmer in size trouble examined his code to see what he could throw over the fence into a neighbor's space. So buffers managed by the control program became part of the user's space. More seriously, so did all kinds of control blocks, and the effect was utterly compromising to the security and protection of the system.

So the second moral is also clear: Define exactly what a module must do when you specify how big it must be.

A third and deeper lesson shows through these experiences. The project was large enough and management communication poor enough to prompt many members of the team to see themselves as contestants making brownie points, rather than as builders making programming products. Each suboptimized his piece to meet his targets; few stopped to think about the total effect on the customer. This breakdown in orientation and communication is a major hazard for large projects. All during implementation, the system architects must maintain continual vigilance to ensure continued system integrity. Beyond this policing mechanism, however, lies the matter of attitude of the implementers themselves. Fostering a total-system, user-oriented attitude may well be the most important function of the programming manager.

Space Techniques

No amount of space budgeting and control can make a program small. That requires invention and craftsmanship.

Obviously, more function means more space, speed being held constant. So the first area of craftsmanship is in trading function for size. Here there comes an early and deep policy question. How much of that choice shall be reserved for the user? One can design a program with many optional features, each of which takes a little space. One can design a generator that will take an option list and tailor a program to it. But for any particular set of options, a more monolithic program would take less space. It's rather like a car; if the map light, cigarette lighter, and clock are priced together as a single option, the package will cost less than if one can choose each separately. So the designer must decide how fine-grained the user choice of options will be.

In designing a system for a range of memory sizes, another basic question arises. A limiting effect keeps the range of suitability from being made arbitrarily wide, even with fine-grained modularity of function. In the smallest system, most modules will be overlaid. A substantial part of the smallest system's resident space must be set aside as a transient or paging area into which other parts are fetched. The size of this determines the size of all modules. And breaking functions into small modules costs both performance and space. So a large system, which can afford a transient area twenty times as large, only saves accesses thereby. It still suffers in both speed and space because the module size is so small. This effect limits the maximum efficient system that can be generated from the modules of a small system.

The second area of craftsmanship is space-time trade-offs. For a given function, the more space, the faster. This is true over an amazingly large range. It is this fact that makes it feasible to set space budgets.

The manager can do two things to help his team make good space-time trade-offs. One is to ensure that they are trained in programming technique, not just left to rely on native wit and previous experience. For a new language or machine this is especially important. The peculiarities of its skillful use need to be learned quickly and shared widely, perhaps with special prizes or praises for new techniques.

The second is to recognize that programming has a technology, and components need to be fabricated. Every project needs a notebook full of good subroutines or macros for queuing, searching, hashing, and sorting. For each such function the notebook should have at least two programs, the quick and the squeezed. The development of such technology is an important realization task that can be done in parallel with system architecture.

Representation Is the Essence of Programming

Beyond craftsmanship lies invention, and it is here that lean, spare, fast programs are born. Almost always these are the result of stategic breakthrough rather than tactical cleverness. Sometimes the strategic breakthrough will be a new algorithm, such as the Cooley-Tukey Fast Fourier Transform or the substitution of an $n \log n$ sort for an n^2 set of comparisons.

Much more often, strategic breakthrough will come from redoing the representation of the data or tables. This is where the heart of a program lies. Show me your flowcharts and conceal your tables, and I shall continue to be mystified. Show me your tables, and I won't usually need your flowcharts; they'll be obvious.

It is easy to multiply examples of the power of representations. I recall a young man undertaking to build an elaborate console interpreter for an IBM 650. He ended up packing it onto an incredibly small amount of space by building an interpreter for the interpreter, recognizing that human interactions are slow and infrequent, but space was dear. Digitek's elegant little Fortran compiler uses a very dense, specialized representation for the compiler code itself, so that external storage is not needed. That time lost in decoding this representation is gained back tenfold by avoiding input-output. (The exercises at the end of Chapter 6 in Brooks and Iverson, *Automatic Data Processing*[1] include a collection of such examples, as do many of Knuth's exercises.[2])

The programmer at wit's end for lack of space can often do best by disentangling himself from his code, rearing back, and contemplating his data. Representation *is* the essence of programming.

10
The Documentary Hypothesis

10
The Documentary Hypothesis

The hypothesis:

Amid a wash of paper, a small number of documents become the critical pivots around which every project's management revolves. These are the manager's chief personal tools.

W. Bengough, "Scene in the old Congressional Library," 1897
The Bettman Archive

The technology, the surrounding organization, and the traditions of the craft conspire to define certain items of paperwork that a project must prepare. To the new manager, fresh from operating as a craftsman himself, these seem an unmitigated nuisance, an unnecessary distraction, and a white tide that threatens to engulf him. And indeed, most of them are exactly that.

Bit by bit, however, he comes to realize that a certain small set of these documents embodies and expresses much of his managerial work. The preparation of each one serves as a major occasion for focusing thought and crystallizing discussions that otherwise would wander endlessly. Its maintenance becomes his surveillance and warning mechanism. The document itself serves as a check list, a status control, and a data base for his reporting.

In order to see how this should work for a software project, let us examine the specific documents useful in other contexts and see if a generalization emerges.

Documents for a Computer Product

Suppose one is building a machine. What are the critical documents?

Objectives. This defines the need to be met and the goals, desiderata, constraints, and priorities.

Specifications. This is a computer manual plus performance specifications. It is one of the first documents generated in proposing a new product, and the last document finished.

Schedule

Budget. Not merely a constraint, the budget is one of the manager's most useful documents. Existence of the budget forces technical decisions that otherwise would be avoided; and, more important, it forces and clarifies policy decisions.

Organization chart

Space allocations

Estimate, forecast, prices.   These three have cyclic interlocking, which determines the success or failure of the project:

To generate a market forecast, one needs performance specifications and postulated prices. The quantities from the forecast combine with component counts from the design to determine the manufacturing cost estimate, and they determine the per-unit share of development and fixed costs. These costs in turn determine prices.

If the prices are *below* those postulated, a joyous success spiral begins. Forecasts rise, unit costs drop, and prices drop yet further.

If the prices are *above* those postulated, a disastrous spiral begins, and all hands must struggle to break it. Performance must be squeezed up and new applications developed to support larger forecasts. Costs must be squeezed down to yield lower estimates. The stress of this cycle is a discipline that often evokes the best work of marketer and engineer.

It can also bring about ridiculous vacillation. I recall a machine whose instruction counter popped in or out of memory every six months during a three-year development cycle. At one phase a little more performance would be wanted, so the instruction counter was implemented in transistors. At the next phase cost reduction was the theme, so the counter would be implemented as a memory location. On another project the best engineering manager I ever saw served often as a giant flywheel, his inertia damping the fluctuations that came from market and management people.

Documents for a University Department

In spite of the immense differences in purpose and activity, a similar number of similar documents form the critical set for the chairman of a university department. Almost every decision by dean, faculty meeting, or chairman is a specification or change of these documents:

Objectives

Course descriptions

Degree requirements

Research proposals (hence plans, when funded)

Class schedule and teaching assignments

Budget

Space allocation

Assignment of staff and graduate students

Notice that the components are very like those of the computer project: objectives, product specifications, time allocations, money allocations, space allocations, and people allocations. Only the pricing documents are missing; here the legislature does that task. The similarities are not accidental—the concerns of any management task are what, when, how much, where, and who.

Documents for a Software Project

In many software projects, people begin by holding meetings to debate structure; then they start writing programs. No matter how small the project, however, the manager is wise to begin immediately to formalize at least mini-documents to serve as his data base. And he turns out to need documents much like those of other managers.

What: objectives.   This defines the need to be met and the goals, desiderata, constraints, and priorities.

What: product specifications.   This begins as a proposal and ends up as the manual and internal documentation. Speed and space specifications are a critical part.

When: schedule

How much: budget

Where: space allocation

Who: organization chart. This becomes intertwined with the interface specification, as Conway's Law predicts: "Organizations which design systems are constrained to produce systems which are copies of the communication structures of these organizations."[1] Conway goes on to point out that the organization chart will initially reflect the first system design, which is almost surely not the right one. If the system design is to be free to change, the organization must be prepared to change.

Why Have Formal Documents?

First, writing the decisions down is essential. Only when one writes do the gaps appear and the inconsistencies protrude. The act of writing turns out to require hundreds of mini-decisions, and it is the existence of these that distinguishes clear, exact policies from fuzzy ones.

Second, the documents will communicate the decisions to others. The manager will be continually amazed that policies he took for common knowledge are totally unknown by some member of his team. Since his fundamental job is to keep everybody going in the same direction, his chief daily task will be communication, not decision-making, and his documents will immensely lighten this load.

Finally, a manager's documents give him a data base and checklist. By reviewing them periodically he sees where he is, and he sees what changes of emphasis or shifts in direction are needed.

I do not share the salesman-projected vision of the "management total-information system," wherein the executive strokes an inquiry into a computer, and a display screen flashes his answer. There are many fundamental reasons why this will never happen.

One reason is that only a small part—perhaps 20 percent—of the executive's time is spent on tasks where he needs information from outside his head. The rest is communication: hearing, reporting, teaching, exhorting, counseling, encouraging. But for the fraction that *is* data-based, the handful of critical documents are vital, and they will meet almost all needs.

The task of the manager is to develop a plan and then to realize it. But only the written plan is precise and communicable. Such a plan consists of documents on what, when, how much, where, and who. This small set of critical documents encapsulates much of the manager's work. If their comprehensive and critical nature is recognized in the beginning, the manager can approach them as friendly tools rather than annoying busywork. He will set his direction much more crisply and quickly by doing so.

11
Plan to Throw
One Away

11
Plan to Throw
One Away

There is nothing in this world constant but inconstancy.

SWIFT

It is common sense to take a method and try it. If it fails, admit it frankly and try another. But above all, try something.

FRANKLIN D. ROOSEVELT[1]

Collapse of the aerodynamically misdesigned Tacoma Narrows Bridge, 1940
UPI Photo

Pilot Plants and Scaling Up

Chemical engineers learned long ago that a process that works in the laboratory cannot be implemented in a factory in only one step. An intermediate step called the *pilot plant* is necessary to give experience in scaling quantities up and in operating in nonprotective environments. For example, a laboratory process for desalting water will be tested in a pilot plant of 10,000 gallon/day capacity before being used for a 2,000,000 gallon/day community water system.

Programming system builders have also been exposed to this lesson, but it seems to have not yet been learned. Project after project designs a set of algorithms and then plunges into construction of customer-deliverable software on a schedule that demands delivery of the first thing built.

In most projects, the first system built is barely usable. It may be too slow, too big, awkward to use, or all three. There is no alternative but to start again, smarting but smarter, and build a redesigned version in which these problems are solved. The discard and redesign may be done in one lump, or it may be done piece-by-piece. But all large-system experience shows that it will be done.[2] Where a new system concept or new technology is used, one has to build a system to throw away, for even the best planning is not so omniscient as to get it right the first time.

The management question, therefore, is not *whether* to build a pilot system and throw it away. You *will* do that. The only question is whether to plan in advance to build a throwaway, or to promise to deliver the throwaway to customers. Seen this way, the answer is much clearer. Delivering that throwaway to customers buys time, but it does so only at the cost of agony for the user, distraction for the builders while they do the redesign, and a bad reputation for the product that the best redesign will find hard to live down.

Hence *plan to throw one away; you will, anyhow.*

The Only Constancy Is Change Itself

Once one recognizes that a pilot system must be built and discarded, and that a redesign with changed ideas is inevitable, it becomes useful to face the whole phenomenon of change. The first step is to accept the fact of change as a way of life, rather than an untoward and annoying exception. Cosgrove has perceptively pointed out that the programmer delivers satisfaction of a user need rather than any tangible product. And both the actual need and the user's perception of that need will change as programs are built, tested, and used.[3]

Of course this is also true of the needs met by hardware products, whether new cars or new computers. But the very existence of a tangible object serves to contain and quantize user demand for changes. Both the tractability and the invisibility of the software product expose its builders to perpetual changes in requirements.

Far be it from me to suggest that all changes in customer objectives and requirements must, can, or should be incorporated in the design. Clearly a threshold has to be established, and it must get higher and higher as development proceeds, or no product ever appears.

Nevertheless, some changes in objectives are inevitable, and it is better to be prepared for them than to assume that they won't come. Not only are changes in objective inevitable, changes in development strategy and technique are also inevitable. The throw-one-away concept is itself just an acceptance of the fact that as one learns, he changes the design.[4]

Plan the System for Change

The ways of designing a system for such change are well known and widely discussed in the literature—perhaps more widely discussed than practiced. They include careful modularization, extensive subroutining, precise and complete definition of intermodule interfaces, and complete documentation of these. Less obviously one wants standard calling sequences and table-driven techniques used wherever possible.

Most important is the use of a high-level language and self-documenting techniques so as to reduce errors induced by changes. Using compile-time operations to incorporate standard declarations helps powerfully in making changes.

Quantization of change is an essential technique. Every product should have numbered versions, and each version must have its own schedule and a freeze date, after which changes go into the next version.

Plan the Organization for Change

Cosgrove advocates treating all plans, milestones, and schedules as tentative, so as to facilitate change. This goes much too far—the common failing of programming groups today is too little management control, not too much.

Nevertheless, he offers a great insight. He observes that the reluctance to document designs is not due merely to laziness or time pressure. Instead it comes from the designer's reluctance to commit himself to the defense of decisions which he knows to be tentative. "By documenting a design, the designer exposes himself to the criticisms of everyone, and he must be able to defend everything he writes. If the organizational structure is threatening in any way, nothing is going to be documented until it is completely defensible."

Structuring an organization for change is much harder than designing a system for change. Each man must be assigned to jobs that broaden him, so that the whole force is technically flexible. On a large project the manager needs to keep two or three top programmers as a technical cavalry that can gallop to the rescue wherever the battle is thickest.

Management structures also need to be changed as the system changes. This means that the boss must give a great deal of attention to keeping his managers and his technical people as interchangeable as their talents allow.

The barriers are sociological, and they must be fought with constant vigilance. First, managers themselves often think of senior people as "too valuable" to use for actual programming. Next, management jobs carry higher prestige. To overcome this problem some laboratories, such as Bell Labs, abolish all job titles. Each professional employee is a "member of the technical staff." Others, like IBM, maintain a dual ladder of advancement, as Fig. 11.1 shows. The corresponding rungs are in theory equivalent.

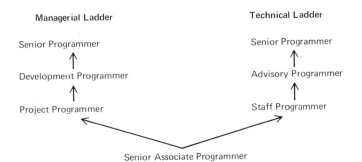

Fig. 11.1   IBM dual ladder of advancement

It is easy to establish corresponding salary scales for rungs. It is much harder to give them corresponding prestige. Offices have to be of equal size and appointment. Secretarial and other support services must correspond. A reassignment from the technical ladder to a corresponding level on the managerial one should never be accompanied by a raise, and it should be announced always as a "reassignment," never as a "promotion." The reverse reassignment should always carry a raise; overcompensating for the cultural forces is necessary.

Managers need to be sent to technical refresher courses, senior technical people to management training. Project objectives, progress, and management problems must be shared with the whole body of senior people.

Whenever talents permit, senior people must be kept technically and emotionally ready to manage groups or to delight in building programs with their own hands. Doing this surely is a lot of work; but it surely is worth it!

The whole notion of organizing surgical-type programming teams is a radical attack on this problem. It has the effect of making a senior man feel that he does not demean himself when he builds programs, and it attempts to remove the social obstacles that deprive him of that creative joy.

Furthermore, that structure is designed to minimize the number of interfaces. As such, it makes the system maximally easy to change, and it becomes relatively easy to reassign a whole surgical team to a different programming task when organizational changes are necessary. It is really the long-run answer to the problem of flexible organization.

Two Steps Forward and One Step Back

A program doesn't stop changing when it is delivered for customer use. The changes after delivery are called *program maintenance,* but the process is fundamentally different from hardware maintenance.

Hardware maintenance for a computer system involves three activities—replacing deteriorated components, cleaning and lubricating, and putting in engineering changes that fix design defects. (Most, but not all, engineering changes fix defects in the realization or implementation, rather than the architecture, and so are invisible to the user.)

Program maintenance involves no cleaning, lubrication, or repair of deterioration. It consists chiefly of changes that repair design defects. Much more often than with hardware, these changes include added functions. Usually they are visible to the user.

The total cost of maintaining a widely used program is typically 40 percent or more of the cost of developing it. Surprisingly, this cost is strongly affected by the number of users. More users find more bugs.

Betty Campbell, of MIT's Laboratory for Nuclear Science, points out an interesting cycle in the life of a particular release of a program. It is shown in Fig. 11.2. Initially, old bugs found and solved in previous releases tend to reappear in a new release. New functions of the new release turn out to have defects. These things get shaken out, and all goes well for several months. Then the bug rate begins to climb again. Miss Campbell believes this is due to the arrival of users at a new plateau of sophistication, where they begin to exercise fully the new capabilities of the release. This intense workout then smokes out the more subtle bugs in the new features.[5]

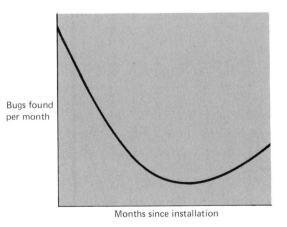

Bugs found per month

Months since installation

Fig. 11.2   Bug occurrence as a function of release age

The fundamental problem with program maintenance is that fixing a defect has a substantial (20–50 percent) chance of introducing another. So the whole process is two steps forward and one step back.

Why aren't defects fixed more cleanly? First, even a subtle defect shows itself as a local failure of some kind. In fact it often has system-wide ramifications, usually nonobvious. Any attempt to fix it with minimum effort will repair the local and obvious, but unless the structure is pure or the documentation very fine, the far-reaching effects of the repair will be overlooked. Second, the repairer is usually not the man who wrote the code, and often he is a junior programmer or trainee.

As a consequence of the introduction of new bugs, program maintenance requires far more system testing per statement written than any other programming. Theoretically, after each fix one must run the entire bank of test cases previously run against the system, to ensure that it has not been damaged in an obscure way. In practice such *regression testing* must indeed approximate this theoretical ideal, and it is very costly.

Clearly, methods of designing programs so as to eliminate or at least illuminate side effects can have an immense payoff in maintenance costs. So can methods of implementing designs with fewer people, fewer interfaces, and hence fewer bugs.

One Step Forward and One Step Back

Lehman and Belady have studied the history of successive releases in a large operating system.[6] They find that the total number of modules increases linearly with release number, but that the number of modules affected increases exponentially with release number. All repairs tend to destroy the structure, to increase the entropy and disorder of the system. Less and less effort is spent on fixing original design flaws; more and more is spent on fixing flaws introduced by earlier fixes. As time passes, the system becomes less and less well-ordered. Sooner or later the fixing ceases to gain any ground. Each forward step is matched by a backward one. Although in principle usable forever, the system has worn out as a base for progress. Furthermore, machines change, configurations change, and user requirements change, so the system is not in fact usable forever. A brand-new, from-the-ground-up redesign is necessary.

And so from a statistical mechanical model, Belady and Lehman arrive for programming-systems at a more general conclusion supported by the experience of all the earth. "Things are always at their best in the beginning," said Pascal. C. S. Lewis has stated it more perceptively:

> *That is the key to history. Terrific energy is expended—civilizations are built up—excellent institutions devised; but each time something goes wrong. Some fatal flaw always brings the selfish and cruel people to the top, and then it all slides back into misery and ruin. In fact, the machine conks. It seems to start up all right and runs a few yards, and then it breaks down.*[7]

Systems program building is an entropy-decreasing process, hence inherently metastable. Program maintenance is an entropy-increasing process, and even its most skillful execution only delays the subsidence of the system into unfixable obsolescence.

12
Sharp Tools

12
Sharp Tools

A good workman is known by his tools.

PROVERB

A. Pisano, "Lo Scultore," from the Campanile di Santa Maria del Fiore, Florence, c. 1335
Scala, New York/Firenze and Foto Alinari, Firenze

Even at this late date, many programming projects are still oper-
ated like machine shops so far as tools are concerned. Each master
mechanic has his own personal set, collected over a lifetime and
carefully locked and guarded—the visible evidences of personal
skills. Just so, the programmer keeps little editors, sorts, binary
dumps, disk space utilities, etc., stashed away in his file.

Such an approach, however, is foolish for a programming
project. First, the essential problem is communication, and indi-
vidualized tools hamper rather than aid communication. Second,
the technology changes when one changes machines or working
language, so tool lifetime is short. Finally, it is obviously much
more efficient to have common development and maintenance of
the general-purpose programming tools.

General-purpose tools are not enough, however. Both specialized needs and personal preferences dictate the need for specialized tools as well; so in discussing programming teams I have
postulated one toolmaker per team. This man masters all the common tools and is able to instruct his client-boss in their use. He
also builds the specialized tools his boss needs.

The manager of a project, then, needs to establish a philosophy and set aside resources for the building of common tools. At
the same time he must recognize the need for specialized tools, and
not begrudge his working teams their own tool-building. This
temptation is insidious. One feels that if all those scattered tool
builders were gathered in to augment the common tool team,
greater efficiency would result. But it is not so.

What are the tools about which the manager must philoso-
phize, plan, and organize? First, a *computer facility.* This requires
machines, and a scheduling philosophy must be adopted. It requires an *operating system,* and service philosophies must be established. It requires *language,* and a language policy must be laid
down. Then there are *utilities, debugging aids, test-case generators,*
and a *text-processing system* to handle documentation. Let us look
at these one by one.[1]

Target Machines

Machine support is usefully divided into the *target machine* and the *vehicle machines.* The target machine is the one for which software is being written, and on which it must ultimately be tested. The vehicle machines are those that provide the services used in building the system. If one is building a new operating system for an old machine, it may serve not only as the target, but as the vehicle as well.

What kind of target facility?   Teams building new supervisors or other system-heart software will of course need machines of their own. Such systems will need operators and a system programmer or two who keeps the standard support on the machine current and serviceable.

If a separate machine is needed, it is a rather peculiar thing— it need not be fast, but it needs at least a million bytes of main storage, a hundred million bytes of on-line disk, and terminals. Only alphanumeric terminals are needed, but they must go much faster than the 15 characters per second that characterizes typewriters. A large memory adds greatly to productivity by allowing overlaying and size trimming to be done after functional testing.

The debugging machine, or its software, also needs to be instrumented, so that counts and measurements of all kinds of program parameters can be automatically made during debugging. Memory-use patterns, for instance, are powerful diagnostics of the causes of weird logical behavior or unexpectedly slow performance.

Scheduling.   When the target machine is new, as when its first operating system is being built, machine time is scarce, and scheduling it is a major problem. The requirement for target machine time has a peculiar growth curve. In OS/360 development we had good System/360 simulators and other vehicles. From previous experience we projected how many hours of S/360 time we would need, and began to acquire early machines from factory production. But they sat idle, month after month. Then all at once all 16 systems were fully loaded, and rationing was the problem. The utilization looked something like Fig. 12.1. Everyone began to debug his first components at the same time, and thereafter most of the team was constantly debugging something.

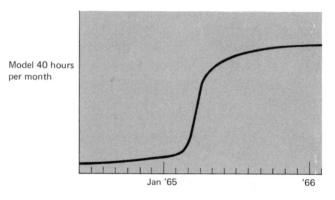

Model 40 hours
per month

Jan '65   '66

Fig. 12.1   Growth in use of target machines

We centralized all our machines and tape library and set up a professional and experienced machine-room team to run them. To maximize scarce S/360 time, we ran all debugging runs in batch on whichever system was free and appropriate. We tried for four shots per day (two-and-one-half-hour turnaround) and demanded four-hour turnaround. An auxiliary 1401 with terminals was used to schedule runs, to keep track of the thousands of jobs, and to monitor turnaround time.

But all that organization was quite overdone. After a few months of slow turnaround, mutual recriminations, and other agony, we went to allocating machine time in substantial blocks.

The whole fifteen-man sort team, for example, would be given a system for a four-to-six-hour block. It was up to them to schedule themselves on it. If it sat idle, no outsider could use it.

That, it develops, was a better way to allocate and schedule. Although machine utilization may have been a little lower (and often it wasn't), productivity was way up. For each man on such a team, ten shots in a six-hour block are far more productive than ten shots spaced three hours apart, because sustained concentration reduces thinking time. After such a sprint, a team usually needed a day or two to catch up on the paperwork before asking for another block. Often as few as three programmers can fruitfully share and subschedule a block of time. This seems to be the best way to use a target machine when debugging a new operating system.

It has always been so in practice, though never in theory. System debugging has always been a graveyard-shift occupation, like astronomy. Twenty years ago, on the 701, I was initiated into the productive informality of the predawn hours, when all the machine-room bosses are fast asleep at home, and the operators are disinclined to be sticklers for rules. Three machine generations have passed; technologies have changed totally; operating systems have arisen; and yet this preferred method of working hasn't changed. It endures because it is most productive. The time has come to recognize its productivity and embrace the fruitful practice openly.

Vehicle Machines and Data Services

Simulators.   If the target computer is new, one needs a logical simulator for it. This gives a debugging vehicle long before the real target exists. Equally important, it gives access to a *dependable* debugging vehicle even after one has a target machine available.

Dependable is not the same as *accurate.* The simulator will surely fail in some respect to be a faithful and accurate implementation of the new machine's architecture. But it will be the *same* implementation from one day to the next, and the new hardware will not.

We are accustomed nowadays to having computer hardware work correctly almost all the time. Unless an application programmer sees a system behaving inconsistently from run to identical run, he is well advised to look for bugs in his code rather than in his engine.

This experience, however, is bad training for the programming of support for a new machine. Lab-built, preproduction, or early hardware does *not* work as defined, does *not* work reliably, and does *not* stay the same from day to day. As bugs are found, engineering changes are made in all machine copies, including those of the programming group. This shifting base is bad enough. Hardware failures, usually intermittent, are worse. The uncertainty is worst of all, for it robs one of incentive to dig diligently in his code for a bug—it may not be there at all. So a dependable simulator on a well-aged vehicle retains its usefulness far longer than one would expect.

Compiler and assembler vehicles. For the same reasons, one wants compilers and assemblers that run on dependable vehicles but compile object code for the target system. This can then start being debugged on the simulator.

With high-level language programming, one can do much of the debugging by compiling for and testing object code on the vehicle machine before beginning to test target-machine code at all. This gives the efficiency of direct execution, rather than that of simulation, combined with the dependability of the stable machine.

Program libraries and accounting. A very successful and important use of a vehicle machine in the OS/360 development effort was for the maintenance of program libraries. A system developed under the leadership of W. R. Crowley had two 7010's connected, sharing a large disk data bank. The 7010's also provided an S/360 assembler. All the code tested or under test was kept in this library, both source code and assembled load modules. The library was in fact divided into sublibraries with different access rules.

First, each group or programmer had an area where he kept copies of his programs, his test cases, and the scaffolding he needed for component testing. In this *playpen* area there were no restrictions on what a man could do with his own programs; they were his.

When a man had his component ready for integration into a larger piece, he passed a copy over to the manager of that larger system, who put this copy into a *system integration sublibrary*. Now the original programmer could not change it, except by permission of the integration manager. As the system came together, the latter would proceed with all sorts of system tests, identifying bugs and getting fixes.

From time to time a system version would be ready for wider use. Then it would be promoted to the *current version sublibrary*. This copy was sacrosanct, touched only to fix crippling bugs. It was available for use in integration and testing of all new module versions. A program directory on the 7010 kept track of each version of each module, its status, its whereabouts, and its changes.

Two notions are important here. The first is *control,* the idea of program copies belonging to managers who alone can authorize their change. The second is that of *formal separation* and *progression* from the playpen, to integration, to release.

In my opinion this was one of the best-done things in the OS/360 effort. It is a piece of management technology that seems to have been independently developed on several massive programming projects including those at Bell Labs, ICL, and Cambridge University.[2] It is applicable to documentation as well as to programs. It is an indispensable technology.

Program tools. As new debugging techniques appear, the old ones diminish but do not vanish. Thus one needs dumps, source-file editors, snapshot dumps, even traces.

Likewise one needs a full set of utilities for putting decks on disks, making tape copies, printing files, changing catalogs. If one commissions a project toolmaker early in the process, these can be done once and can be ready by time they are needed.

Documentation system.   Among all tools, the one that saves the most labor may well be a computerized text-editing system, operating on a dependable vehicle. We had a very handy one, devised by J. W. Franklin. Without it I expect OS/360 manuals would have been far later and more cryptic. There are those who would argue that the OS/360 six-foot shelf of manuals represents verbal diarrhea, that the very voluminosity introduces a new kind of incomprehensibility. And there is some truth in that.

But I respond in two ways. First, the OS/360 documentation is overwhelming in bulk, but the reading plan is carefully laid out; if one uses it selectively, he can ignore most of the bulk most of the time. One must consider the OS/360 documentation as a library or an encyclopedia, not a set of mandatory texts.

Second, this is far preferable to the severe underdocumentation that characterizes most programming systems. I will quickly agree, however, that the writing could be vastly improved in some places, and that the result of better writing would be reduced bulk. Some parts (e.g., *Concepts and Facilities*) are very well-written now.

Performance simulator.   Better have one. Build it outside-in, as we will discuss in the next chapter. Use the same top-down design for the performance simulator, the logical simulator, and the product. Start it very early. Listen to it when it speaks.

High-Level Language and Interactive Programming

The most important two tools for system programming today are two that were not used in OS/360 development almost a decade ago. They are still not widely used, but all evidence points to their power and applicability. They are (1) high-level language and (2) interactive programming. I am convinced that only inertia and sloth prevent the universal adoption of these tools; the technical difficulties are no longer valid excuses.

High-level language.   The chief reasons for using a high-level language are productivity and debugging speed. We have discussed productivity earlier (Chapter 8). There is not a lot of numerical evidence, but what there is suggests improvement by integral factors, not just incremental percentages.

The debugging improvement comes from the fact that there are fewer bugs, and they are easier to find. There are fewer because one avoids an entire level of exposure to error, a level on which one makes not only syntactic errors but semantic ones, such as misusing registers. The bugs are easier to find because the compiler diagnostics help find them and, more important, because it is very easy to insert debugging snapshots.

For me, these productivity and debugging reasons are overwhelming. I cannot easily conceive of a programming system I would build in assembly language.

Well, what about the classical objections to such a tool? There are three: It doesn't let me do what I want. The object code is too big. The object code is too slow.

As to function, I believe the objection is no longer valid. All testimony indicates that one can do what he needs to do, but that it takes work to find out how, and one may occasionally need unlovely artifices.[3,4]

As to space, the new optimizing compilers are beginning to be very satisfactory, and this improvement will continue.

As to speed, optimizing compilers now produce some code that is faster than most programmer's handwritten code, Furthermore, one can usually solve speed problems by replacing from one to five percent of a compiler-generated program by handwritten substitute after the former is fully debugged.[5]

What high-level language should one use for system programming? The only reasonable candidate today is PL/I.[6] It has a very full set of functions; it is matched to operating system environments; and a variety of compilers are available, some interactive, some fast, some very diagnostic, and some producing highly optimized code. I myself find it faster to work out algorithms in APL; then I translate these to PL/I for matching to the system environment.

Interactive programming.   One of the justifications for MIT's Multics project was its usefulness for building programming systems. Multics (and following it, IBM's TSS) differs in concept from other interactive computing systems in exactly those respects necessary for systems programming: many levels of sharing and protection for data and programs, extensive library management, and facilities for cooperative work among terminal users. I am convinced that interactive systems will never displace batch systems for many applications. But I think the Multics team has made its most convincing case in the system-programming application.

There is not yet much evidence available on the true fruitfulness of such apparently powerful tools. There *is* a widespread recognition that debugging is the hard and slow part of system programming, and slow turnaround is the bane of debugging. So the logic of interactive programming seems inexorable.[7]

Program	Size	Batch (B) or Conversational (C)	Instructions/man-year
ESS code	800,000	B	500-1000
7094 ESS support	120,000	B	2100-3400
360 ESS support	32,000	C	8000
360 ESS support	8,300	B	4000

Fig. 12.2 Comparative productivity under batch and conversational programming

Further, we hear good testimonies from many who have built little systems or parts of systems in this way. The only numbers I have seen for effects on programming of large systems were reported by John Harr of Bell Labs. They are shown in Fig. 12.2. These numbers are for writing, assembling, and debugging programs. The first program is mostly control program; the other three are language translators, editors, and such. Harr's data suggest that an interactive facility at least doubles productivity in system programming.[8]

The effective use of most interactive tools requires that the work be done in a high-level language, for teletype and typewriter terminals cannot be used to debug by dumping memory. With a high-level language, source can be easily edited and selective printouts easily done. Together they make a pair of sharp tools indeed.

13
The Whole and the Parts

13
The Whole and the Parts

I can call spirits from the vasty deep.

Why so can I, or so can any man; but will they come
when you do call for them?

SHAKESPEARE, KING HENRY IV, PART I

The modern magic, like the old, has its boastful practitioners: "I can write programs that control air traffic, intercept ballistic missiles, reconcile bank accounts, control production lines." To which the answer comes, "So can I, and so can any man, but do they work when you do write them?"

How does one build a program to work? How does one test a program? And how does one integrate a tested set of component programs into a tested and dependable system? We have touched upon the techniques here and there; let us now consider them somewhat more systematically.

Designing the Bugs Out

Bug-proofing the definition.   The most pernicious and subtle bugs are system bugs arising from mismatched assumptions made by the authors of various components. The approach to conceptual integrity discussed above in Chapters 4, 5, and 6 addresses these problems directly. In short, conceptual integrity of the product not only makes it easier to use, it also makes it easier to build and less subject to bugs.

So does the detailed, painstaking architectural effort implied by that approach. V. A. Vyssotsky, of Bell Telephone Laboratories' Safeguard Project, says, "The crucial task is to get the product defined. Many, many failures concern exactly those aspects that were never quite specified."[1] Careful function definition, careful specification, and the disciplined exorcism of frills of function and flights of technique all reduce the number of system bugs that have to be found.

Testing the specification.   Long before any code exists, the specification must be handed to an outside testing group to be scrutinized for completeness and clarity. As Vyssotsky says, the developers themselves cannot do this: "They won't tell you they don't understand it; they will happily invent their way through the gaps and obscurities."

Top-down design. In a very clear 1971 paper, Niklaus Wirth formalized a design procedure which had been used for years by the best programmers.[2] Furthermore, his notions, although stated for program design, apply completely to the design of complex systems of programs. The division of system building into architecture, implementation, and realization is an embodiment of these notions; furthermore, each of the architecture, implementation, and realization can be best done by top-down methods.

Briefly, Wirth's procedure is to identify design as a sequence of *refinement steps.* One sketches a rough task definition and a rough solution method that achieves the principal result. Then one examines the definition more closely to see how the result differs from what is wanted, and one takes the large steps of the solution and breaks them down into smaller steps. Each refinement in the definition of the task becomes a refinement in the algorithm for solution, and each may be accompanied by a refinement in the data representation.

From this process one identifies *modules* of solution or of data whose further refinement can proceed independently of other work. The degree of this modularity determines the adaptability and changeability of the program.

Wirth advocates using as high-level a notation as is possible at each step, exposing the concepts and concealing the details until further refinement becomes necessary.

A good top-down design avoids bugs in several ways. First, the clarity of structure and representation makes the precise statement of requirements and functions of the modules easier. Second, the partitioning and independence of modules avoids system bugs. Third, the suppression of detail makes flaws in the structure more apparent. Fourth, the design can be tested at each of its refinement steps, so testing can start earlier and focus on the proper level of detail at each step.

The process of step-wise refinement does not mean that one never has to go back, scrap the top level, and start the whole thing again as he encounters some unexpectedly knotty detail. Indeed, that happens often. But it is much easier to see exactly when and why one should throw away a gross design and start over. Many poor systems come from an attempt to salvage a bad basic design and patch it with all kinds of cosmetic relief. Top-down design reduces the temptation.

I am persuaded that top-down design is the most important new programming formalization of the decade.

Structured programming.   Another important set of new ideas for designing the bugs out of programs derives largely from Dijkstra,[3] and is built on a theoretical structure by Böhm and Jacopini.[4]

Basically the approach is to design programs whose control structures consist only of loops defined by a statement such as DO WHILE, and conditional portions delineated into groups of statements marked with brackets and conditioned by an IF . . . THEN . . . ELSE. Böhm and Jacopini show these structures to be theoretically sufficient; Dijkstra argues that the alternative, unrestrained branching via GO TO, produces structures that lend themselves to logical errors.

The basic notion is surely sound. Many criticisms have been made, and additional control structures, such as an n-way branch (the so-called CASE statement) for distinguishing among many contingencies, and a disaster bail-out (GO TO ABNORMAL END) are very convenient. Further, some have become very doctrinaire about avoiding all GO TO's, and that seems excessive.

The important point, and the one vital to constructing bug-free programs, is that one wants to think about the control structures of a system as control structures, not as individual branch statements. This way of thinking is a major step forward.

Component Debugging

The procedures for debugging programs have been through a great cycle in the past twenty years, and in some ways they are back where they started. The cycle has gone through four steps, and it is fun to trace them and see the motivation for each.

On-machine debugging.   Early machines had relatively poor input-output equipment, and long input-output delays. Typically, the machine read and wrote paper tape or magnetic tape and off-line facilities were used for tape preparation and printing. This made tape input-output intolerably awkward for debugging, so the console was used instead. Thus debugging was designed to allow as many trials as possible per machine session.

The programmer carefully designed his debugging procedure —planning where to stop, what memory locations to examine, what do find there, and what to do if he didn't. This meticulous programming of himself as a debugging machine might well take half as long as writing the computer program to be debugged.

The cardinal sin was to push START boldly without having segmented the program into test sections with planned stops.

Memory dumps.   On-machine debugging was very effective. In a two-hour session, one could get perhaps a dozen shots. But computers were very scarce, and very costly, and the thought of all that machine time going to waste was horrifying.

So when high-speed printers were attached on-line, the technique changed. One ran a program until a check failed, and then dumped the whole memory. Then began the laborious desk work, accounting for each memory location's contents. The desk time was not much different than that for on-machine debugging; but it occurred after the test run, in deciphering, rather than before, in planning. Debugging for any particular user took much longer, because test shots depended upon batch turnaround time. The whole procedure, however, was designed to minimize computer time use, and to serve as many programmers as possible.

Snapshots.   The machines on which memory dumping was developed had 2000–4000 words, or 8K to 16K bytes of memory. But memory sizes grew by leaps and bounds, and total memory dumping became impractical. So people developed techniques for selective dumping, selective tracing, and for inserting snapshots into programs. The OS/360 TESTRAN is an end-of-the-line in this direction, allowing one to insert snapshots into a program without reassembly or recompilation.

Interactive debugging.   In 1959 Codd and his coworkers[5] and Strachey[6] each reported work aimed at time-shared debugging, a way of achieving both the instant turnaround of on-machine debugging and the efficient machine use of batch debugging. The computer would have multiple programs in memory, ready for execution. A terminal, controlled only by program, would be associated with each program being debugged. Debugging would be under control of a supervisory program. When the programmer at a terminal stopped his program to examine progress or to make changes, the supervisor would run another program, thus keeping the machines busy.

Codd's multiprogramming system was developed, but the emphasis was on throughput enhancement by efficient input-output utilization, and interactive debugging was not implemented. Strachey's ideas were improved and implemented in 1963 in an experimental system for the 7090 by Corbató and colleagues at MIT.[7] This development led to the MULTICS, TSS, and other time-sharing systems of today.

The chief user-perceived differences between on-machine debugging as first practiced and the interactive debugging of today are the facilities made possible by the presence of the supervisory program and its associated language interpreters. One can program and debug in a high-level language. Efficient editing facilities make changes and snapshots easy.

Return to the instant-turnaround capability of on-machine debugging has not yet brought a return to the preplanning of debugging sessions. In a sense such preplanning is not so necessary as before, since machine time doesn't waste away while one sits and thinks.

Nevertheless, Gold's interesting experimental results show that three times as much progress in interactive debugging is made on the first interaction of each session as on subsequent interactions.[8] This strongly suggests that we are not realizing the potential of interaction due to lack of session planning. The time has come to dust off the old on-machine techniques.

I find that proper use of a good terminal system requires two hours at the desk for each two-hour session on the terminal. Half of this time is spent in sweeping up after the last session: updating my debugging log, filing updated program listings in my system notebook, explaining strange phenomena. The other half is spent in preparation: planning changes and improvements and designing detailed tests for next time. Without such planning, it is hard to stay productive for as much as two hours. Without the post-session sweep-up, it is hard to keep the succession of terminal sessions systematic and forward-moving.

Test cases.   As for the design of actual debugging procedures and test cases, Gruenberger has an especially good treatment,[9] and there are shorter treatments in other standard texts. [10,11]

System Debugging

The unexpectedly hard part of building a programming system is system test. I have already discussed some of the reasons for both the difficulty and its unexpectedness. From all of that, one should be convinced of two things: system debugging will take longer than one expects, and its difficulty justifies a thoroughly systematic and planned approach. Let us now see what such an approach involves.[12]

Use debugged components.   Common sense, if not common practice, dictates that one should begin system debugging only after the pieces seem to work.

Common practice departs from this in two ways. First is the bolt-it-together-and-try approach. This seems to be based on the notion that there will be system (i.e., interface) bugs in addition to the component bugs. The sooner one puts the pieces together, the sooner the system bugs will emerge. Somewhat less sophisticated is the notion that by using the pieces to test each other, one avoids a lot of test scaffolding. Both of these are obviously true, but experience shows that they are not the whole truth—the use of clean, debugged components saves much more time in system testing than that spent on scaffolding and thorough component test.

A little more subtle is the "documented bug" approach. This says that a component is ready to enter system test when all the flaws are *found,* well before the time when all are *fixed.* Then in system testing, so the theory goes, one knows the expected effects of these bugs and can ignore those effects, concentrating on the new phenomena.

All this is just wishful thinking, invented to rationalize away the pain of slipped schedules. One does *not* know all the expected effects of known bugs. If things were straightforward, system testing wouldn't be hard. Furthermore, the fixing of the documented component bugs will surely inject unknown bugs, and then system test is confused.

Build plenty of scaffolding.   By scaffolding I mean all programs and data built for debugging purposes but never intended to be in the final product. It is not unreasonable for there to be half as much code in scaffolding as there is in product.

One form of scaffolding is the *dummy component,* which consists only of interfaces and perhaps some faked data or some small test cases. For example, a system may include a sort program which isn't finished yet. Its neighbors can be tested by using a dummy program that merely reads and tests the format of input data, and spews out a set of well-formatted meaningless but ordered data.

Another form is the *miniature file.* A very common form of system bug is misunderstanding of formats for tape and disk files. So it is worthwhile to build some little files that have only a few typical records, but all the descriptions, pointers, etc.

The limiting case of miniature file is the *dummy file,* which really isn't there at all. OS/360's Job Control Language provides such facility, and it is extremely useful for component debugging.

Yet another form of scaffolding are *auxiliary programs.* Generators for test data, special analysis printouts, cross-reference table analyzers, are all examples of the special-purpose jigs and fixtures one may want to build.[13]

Control changes.   Tight control during test is one of the impressive techniques of hardware debugging, and it applies as well to software systems.

First, somebody must be in charge. He and he alone must authorize component changes or substitution of one version for another.

Then, as discussed above, there must be controlled copies of the system: one locked-up copy of the latest versions, used for component testing; one copy under test, with fixes being installed; playpen copies where each man can work away on his component, doing both fixes and extensions.

In System/360 engineering models, one saw occasional strands of purple wire among the routine yellow wires. When a bug was found, two things were done. A quick fix was devised and installed on the system, so testing could proceed. This change was put on in purple wire, so it stuck out like a sore thumb. It was entered in the log. Meanwhile, an official change document was prepared and started into the design automation mill. Eventually this resulted in updated drawings and wire lists, and a new back panel in which the change was implemented in printed circuitry or yellow wire. Now the physical model and the paper were together again, and the purple wire was gone.

Programming needs a purple-wire technique, and it badly needs tight control and deep respect for the paper that ultimately is the product. The vital ingredients of such technique are the logging of all changes in a journal and the distinction, carried conspicuously in source code, between quick patches and thought-through, tested, documented fixes.

Add one component at a time.   This precept, too, is obvious, but optimism and laziness tempt us to violate it. To do it requires dummies and other scaffolding, and that takes work. And after all, perhaps all that work won't be needed? Perhaps there are no bugs?

No! Resist the temptation! That is what systematic system testing is all about. One must assume that there will be lots of bugs, and plan an orderly procedure for snaking them out.

Note that one must have thorough test cases, testing the partial systems after each new piece is added. And the old ones, run successfully on the last partial sum, must be rerun on the new one to test for system regression.

Quantize updates. As the system comes up, the component builders will from time to time appear, bearing hot new versions of their pieces—faster,smaller, more complete, or putatively less buggy. The replacement of a working component by a new version requires the same systematic testing procedure that adding a new component does, although it should require less time, for more complete and efficient test cases will usually be available.

Each team building another component has been using the most recent tested version of the integrated system as a test bed for debugging its piece. Their work will be set back by having that test bed change under them. Of course it must. But the changes need to be quantized. Then each user has periods of productive stability, interrupted by bursts of test-bed change. This seems to be much less disruptive than a constant rippling and trembling.

Lehman and Belady offer evidence that quanta should be very large and widely spaced or else very small and frequent.[14] The latter strategy is more subject to instability, according to their model. My experience confirms it: I would never risk that strategy in practice.

Quantized changes neatly accommodate a purple-wire technique. The quick patch holds until the next regular release of the component, which should incorporate the fix in tested and documented form.

14
Hatching a Catastrophe

14
Hatching a Catastrophe

None love the bearer of bad news.

SOPHOCLES

How does a project get to be a year late?
. . . One day at a time.

A. Canova, "Ercole e Lica," 1802. Hercules hurls to his death the messenger Lycas, who innocently brought the death-garment.

Scala, New York/Firenze and Foto Alinari, Firenze

When one hears of disastrous schedule slippage in a project, he imagines that a series of major calamities must have befallen it. Usually, however, the disaster is due to termites, not tornadoes; and the schedule has slipped imperceptibly but inexorably. Indeed, major calamities are easier to handle; one responds with major force, radical reorganization, the invention of new approaches. The whole team rises to the occasion.

But the day-by-day slippage is harder to recognize, harder to prevent, harder to make up. Yesterday a key man was sick, and a meeting couldn't be held. Today the machines are all down, because lightning struck the building's power transformer. Tomorrow the disk routines won't start testing, because the first disk is a week late from the factory. Snow, jury duty, family problems, emergency meetings with customers, executive audits—the list goes on and on. Each one only postpones some activity by a half-day or a day. And the schedule slips, one day at a time.

Milestones or Millstones?

How does one control a big project on a tight schedule? The first step is to *have* a schedule. Each of a list of events, called milestones, has a date. Picking the dates is an estimating problem, discussed already and crucially dependent on experience.

For picking the milestones there is only one relevant rule. Milestones must be concrete, specific, measurable events, defined with knife-edge sharpness. Coding, for a counterexample, is "90 percent finished" for half of the total coding time. Debugging is "99 percent complete" most of the time. "Planning complete" is an event one can proclaim almost at will.[1]

Concrete milestones, on the other hand, are 100-percent events. "Specifications signed by architects and implementers," "source coding 100 percent complete, keypunched, entered into disk library," "debugged version passes all test cases." These concrete milestones demark the vague phases of planning, coding, debugging.

It is more important that milestones be sharp-edged and un-ambiguous than that they be easily verifiable by the boss. Rarely will a man lie about milestone progress, *if* the milestone is so sharp that he can't deceive himself. But if the milestone is fuzzy, the boss often understands a different report from that which the man gives. To supplement Sophocles, no one enjoys bearing bad news, either, so it gets softened without any real intent to deceive.

Two interesting studies of estimating behavior by government contractors on large-scale development projects show that:

1. Estimates of the length of an activity, made and revised carefully every two weeks before the activity starts, do not significantly change as the start time draws near, no matter how wrong they ultimately turn out to be.
2. *During* the activity, *over*estimates of duration come steadily down as the activity proceeds.
3. *Underestimates* do not change significantly during the activity until about three weeks before the scheduled completion.[2]

Sharp milestones are in fact a service to the team, and one they can properly expect from a manager. The fuzzy milestone is the harder burden to live with. It is in fact a millstone that grinds down morale, for it deceives one about lost time until it is irremediable. And chronic schedule slippage is a morale-killer.

"The Other Piece Is Late, Anyway"

A schedule slips a day; so what? Who gets excited about a one-day slip? We can make it up later. And the other piece into which ours fits is late, anyway.

A baseball manager recognizes a nonphysical talent, *hustle,* as an essential gift of great players and great teams. It is the characteristic of running faster than necessary, moving sooner than necessary, trying harder than necessary. It is essential for great programming teams, too. Hustle provides the cushion, the reserve capacity, that enables a team to cope with routine mishaps, to anticipate and forfend minor calamities. The calculated response, the measured effort, are the wet blankets that dampen hustle. As we have seen, one *must* get excited about a one-day slip. Such are the elements of catastrophe.

But not all one-day slips are equally disastrous. So some calculation of response is necessary, though hustle be dampened. How does one tell which slips matter? There is no substitute for a PERT chart or a critical-path schedule. Such a network shows who waits for what. It shows who is on the critical path, where any slip moves the end date. It also shows how much an activity can slip before it moves into the critical path.

The PERT technique, strictly speaking, is an elaboration of critical-path scheduling in which one estimates three times for every event, times corresponding to different probabilities of meeting the estimated dates. I do not find this refinement to be worth the extra effort, but for brevity I will call any critical path network a PERT chart.

The preparation of a PERT chart is the most valuable part of its use. Laying out the network, identifying the dependencies, and estimating the legs all force a great deal of very specific planning very early in a project. The first chart is always terrible, and one invents and invents in making the second one.

As the project proceeds, the PERT chart provides the answer to the demoralizing excuse, "The other piece is late anyhow." It shows how hustle is needed to keep one's own part off the critical path, and it suggests ways to make up the lost time in the other part.

Under the Rug

When a first-line manager sees his small team slipping behind, he is rarely inclined to run to the boss with this woe. The team might be able to make it up, or he should be able to invent or reorganize to solve the problem. Then why worry the boss with it? So far, so good. Solving such problems is exactly what the first-line manager is there for. And the boss does have enough real worries demanding his action that he doesn't seek others. So all the dirt gets swept under the rug.

But every boss needs two kinds of information, exceptions to plan that require action and a status picture for education.[3] For that purpose he needs to know the status of all his teams. Getting a true picture of that status is hard.

The first-line manager's interests and those of the boss have an inherent conflict here. The first-line manager fears that if he reports his problem, the boss will act on it. Then his action will preempt the manager's function, diminish his authority, foul up his other plans. So as long as the manager thinks he can solve it alone, he doesn't tell the boss.

Two rug-lifting techniques are open to the boss. Both must be used. The first is to reduce the role conflict and inspire sharing of status. The other is to yank the rug back.

Reducing the role conflict.   The boss must first distinguish between action information and status information. He must discipline himself *not* to act on problems his managers can solve, and *never* to act on problems when he is explicitly reviewing status. I once knew a boss who invariably picked up the phone to give orders before the end of the first paragraph in a status report. That response is guaranteed to squelch full disclosure.

Conversely, when the manager knows his boss will accept status reports without panic or preemption, he comes to give honest appraisals.

This whole process is helped if the boss labels meetings, reviews, conferences, as *status-review* meetings versus *problem-action* meetings, and controls himself accordingly. Obviously one may call a problem-action meeting as a consequence of a status meeting, if he believes a problem is out of hand. But at least everybody knows what the score is, and the boss thinks twice before grabbing the ball.

Yanking the rug off.   Nevertheless, it is necessary to have review techniques by which the true status is made known, whether cooperatively or not. The PERT chart with its frequent sharp milestones is the basis for such review. On a large project one may want to review some part of it each week, making the rounds once a month or so.

A report showing milestones and actual completions is the key document. Figure 14.1 shows an excerpt from such a report. This report shows some troubles. Specifications approval is overdue on several components. Manual (SLR) approval is overdue on another, and one is late getting out of the first state (Alpha) of the independently conducted product test. So such a report serves as an agenda for the meeting of 1 February. Everyone knows the questions, and the component manager should be prepared to explain why it's late, when it will be finished, what steps he's taking, and what help, if any, he needs from the boss or collateral groups.

V. Vyssotsky of Bell Telephone Laboratories adds the following observation:

> *I have found it handy to carry both "scheduled" and "estimated" dates in the milestone report. The scheduled dates are the property of the project manager and represent a consistent work plan for the project as a whole, and one which is a priori a reasonable plan. The estimated dates are the property of the lowest level manager who has cognizance over the piece of work in question, and represents his best judgment as to when it will actually happen, given the resources he has available and when he received (or has commitments for delivery of) his prerequisite inputs. The project manager has to keep his fingers off the estimated dates, and put the emphasis on getting accurate, unbiased estimates rather than palatable optimistic estimates or self-protective conservative ones. Once this is clearly established in everyone's mind, the project manager can see quite a ways into the future where he is going to be in trouble if he doesn't do something.* [4]

SYSTEM/360 SUMMARY STATUS REPORT
OS/360 LANGUAGE PROCESSORS + SERVICE PROGRAMS
AS OF FEBRUARY 01, 1965

A=APPROVAL
C=COMPLETED

*=REVISED PLANNED DATE
NE=NOT ESTABLISHED

PROJECT	LOCATION	COMMITMNT ANNOUNCE RELEASE	OBJECTIVE AVAILABLE APPROVED	SPECS AVAILABLE APPROVED	SRL AVAILABLE APPROVED	ALPHA TEST ENTRY EXIT	COMP TEST START COMPLETE	SYS TEST START COMPLETE	BULLETIN AVAILABLE APPROVED	BETA TEST ENTRY EXIT
OPERATING SYSTEM										
12K DESIGN LEVEL (E)										
ASSEMBLY	SAN JOSE	04/--/4 C 12/31/5	10/28/4 A	10/13/4 C 01/11/5	11/13/4 C 11/18/4 A	01/15/5 C 02/22/5				09/01/5 11/30/5
FORTRAN	POK	04/--/4 C 12/31/5	10/28/4 A	10/21/4 C 01/22/5	12/17/4 C 12/19/4 A	01/15/5 C 02/22/5				09/01/5 11/30/5
COBOL	ENDICOTT	04/--/4 C 12/31/5	10/28/4 A	11/15/4 C 01/20/5 A	11/17/4 C 12/08/4 A	01/15/5 A 02/22/5				09/01/5 11/30/5
RPG	SAN JOSE	04/--/4 C 12/31/5	10/28/4 A	09/30/4 C 01/05/5 A	12/02/4 C 01/18/5 A	01/15/5 C 02/22/5				09/01/5 11/30/5
UTILITIES	TIME/LIFE	04/--/4 C 12/31/5	06/24/4 C		11/20/4 C 11/30/4 A					09/01/5 11/30/5
SORT 1	POK	04/--/4 C 12/31/5	10/28/4 A	10/19/4 C 01/11/5	11/12/4 C 11/30/4 A	01/15/5 C 03/22/5				09/01/5 11/30/5
SORT 2	POK	04/--/4 C 06/30/6	10/28/4 A	10/19/4 C 01/11/5	11/12/4 C 11/30/4 A	01/15/5 C 03/22/5				03/01/6 05/30/6
44K DESIGN LEVEL (F)										
ASSEMBLY	SAN JOSE	04/--/4 C 12/31/5	10/28/4 A	10/13/4 C 01/11/5	11/13/4 C 11/18/4 A	02/15/5 C 03/22/5				09/01/5 11/30/5
COBOL	TIME/LIFE	04/--/4 C 06/30/6	10/28/4 A	10/15/4 C 01/20/5	11/17/4 C 12/08/4 A	02/15/5 C 03/22/5				03/01/6 05/30/6
NPL	HURSLEY	04/--/4 C 03/31/6	10/28/4 A							
2250	KINGSTON	03/30/4 C 03/31/6	11/05/4 C	12/08/4 C 01/04/5	01/12/5 C 01/29/5	01/04/5 C 01/29/5				01/03/6 NE
2280	KINGSTON	06/30/4 C 09/30/6	11/05/4 C			04/01/5 C 04/30/5				01/28/6 NE
200K DESIGN LEVEL (H)										
ASSEMBLY	TIME/LIFE		10/28/4 C							
FORTRAN	POK	04/--/4 C 06/30/6	10/28/4 C	10/16/4 C 01/11/5	11/11/4 C 12/10/4 A	02/15/5 C 03/22/5				03/01/6 05/30/6
NPL	HURSLEY	04/--/4 C 03/31/7	10/28/4 C			07/--/5				01/--/7
NPL H	POK	04/--/4 C	03/30/4 C			02/01/5 C 04/01/5				10/15/5 12/15/5

Figure 14.1

The preparation of the PERT chart is a function of the boss and the managers reporting to him. Its updating, revision, and reporting requires the attention of a small (one to three man) staff group which serves as an extension of the boss. Such a *Plans and Controls* team is invaluable for a large project. It has no authority except to ask all the line managers when they will have set or changed milestones, and whether milestones have been met. Since the Plans and Controls group handles all the paperwork, the burden on the line managers is reduced to the essentials—making the decisions.

We had a skilled, enthusiastic, and diplomatic Plans and Controls group, run by A. M. Pietrasanta, who devoted considerable inventive talent to devising effective but unobtrusive control methods. As a result, I found his group to be widely respected and more than tolerated. For a group whose role is inherently that of an irritant, this is quite an accomplishment.

The investment of a modest amount of skilled effort in a Plans and Controls function is very rewarding. It makes far more difference in project accomplishment than if these people worked directly on building the product programs. For the Plans and Controls group is the watchdog who renders the imperceptible delays visible and who points up the critical elements. It is the early warning system against losing a year, one day at a time.

15
The Other Face

15
The Other Face

A reconstruction of Stonehenge, the world's largest undocumented computer.
The Bettman Archive

A computer program is a message from a man to a machine. The rigidly marshaled syntax and the scrupulous definitions all exist to make intention clear to the dumb engine.

But a written program has another face, that which tells its story to the human user. For even the most private of programs, some such communication is necessary; memory will fail the author-user, and he will require refreshing on the details of his handiwork.

How much more vital is the documentation for a public program, whose user is remote from the author in both time and space! For the program product, the other face to the user is fully as important as the face to the machine.

Most of us have quietly excoriated the remote and anonymous author of some skimpily documented program. And many of us have therefore tried to instill in new programmers an attitude about documentation that would inspire for a lifetime, overcoming sloth and schedule pressure. By and large we have failed. I think we have used wrong methods.

Thomas J. Watson, Sr. told the story of his first experience as a cash register salesman in upstate New York. Charged with enthusiasm, he sallied out with his wagon loaded with cash registers. He worked his territory diligently but without selling a one. Downcast, he reported to his boss. The sales manager listened a while, then said, "Help me load some registers into the wagon, harness the horse, and let's go again." They did, and the two called on customer after customer, with the older man *showing how* to sell cash registers. All evidence indicates that the lesson took.

For several years I diligently lectured my software engineering class on the necessity and propriety of good documentation, exhorting them ever more fervently and eloquently. It didn't work. I assumed they had learned how to document properly and were failing from lack of zeal. Then I tried loading some cash registers into the wagon; i.e., *showing* them how the job is done. This has been much more successful. So the remainder of this essay will downplay exhortation and concentrate on the "how" of good documentation.

What Documentation Is Required?

Different levels of documentation are required for the casual user of a program, for the user who must depend upon a program, and for the user who must adapt a program for changes in circumstance or purpose.

To use a program.   Every user needs a prose description of the program. Most documentation fails in giving too little overview. The trees are described, the bark and leaves are commented, but there is no map of the forest. To write a useful prose description, stand way back and come in slowly:

1. *Purpose.* What is the main function, the reason for the program?
2. *Environment.* On what machines, hardware configurations, and operating system configurations will it run?
3. *Domain and range.* What domain of input is valid? What range of output can legitimately appear?
4. *Functions realized and algorithms used.* Precisely what does it do?
5. *Input-output formats,.* precise and complete.
6. *Operating instructions,* including normal and abnormal ending behavior, as seen at the console and on the outputs.
7. *Options.* What choices does the user have about functions? Exactly how are those choices specified?
8. *Running time.* How long does it take to do a problem of specified size on a specified configuration?
9. *Accuracy and checking.* How precise are the answers expected to be? What means of checking accuracy are incorporated?

Often all this information can be set forth in three or four pages. That requires close attention to conciseness and precision. Most of this document needs to be drafted before the program is written, for it embodies basic planning decisions.

To believe a program.   The description of how it is used must be supplemented with some description of how one knows it is working. This means test cases.

Every copy of a program shipped should include some small test cases that can be routinely used to reassure the user that he has a faithful copy, accurately loaded into the machine.

Then one needs more thorough test cases, which are normally run only after a program is modified. These fall into three parts of the input data domain:

1. Mainline cases that test the program's chief functions for commonly encountered data.
2. Barely legitimate cases that probe the edge of the input data domain, ensuring that largest possible values, smallest possible values, and all kinds of valid exceptions work.
3. Barely illegitimate cases that probe the domain boundary from the other side, ensuring that invalid inputs raise proper diagnostic messages.

To modify a program.   Adapting a program or fixing it requires considerably more information. Of course the full detail is required, and that is contained in a well-commented listing. For the modifier, as well as the more casual user, the crying need is for a clear, sharp overview, this time of the internal structure. What are the components of such an overview?

1. A flow chart or subprogram structure graph. More on this later.
2. Complete descriptions of the algorithms used, or else references to such descriptions in the literature.
3. An explanation of the layout of all files used.
4. An overview of the pass structure—the sequence in which data or programs are brought from tape or disk—and what is accomplished on each pass.
5. A discussion of modifications contemplated in the original design, the nature and location of hooks and exits, and discursive discussion of the ideas of the original author about what modifications might be desirable and how one might proceed. His observations on hidden pitfalls are also useful.

The Flow-Chart Curse

The flow chart is a most thoroughly oversold piece of program documentation. Many programs don't need flow charts at all; few programs need more than a one-page flow chart.

Flow charts show the decision structure of a program, which is only one aspect of its structure. They show decision structure rather elegantly when the flow chart is on one page, but the over-

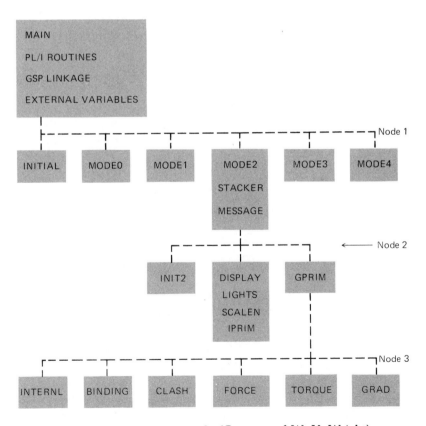

Fig. 15.1 A program structure graph. (Courtesy of W. V. Wright)

view breaks down badly when one has multiple pages, sewed together with numbered exits and connectors.

The one-page flow chart for a substantial program becomes essentially a diagram of program structure, and of phases or steps. As such it is very handy. Figure 15.1 shows such a subprogram structure graph.

Of course such a structure graph neither follows nor needs the painfully wrought ANSI flow-charting standards. All the rules on box shapes, connectors, numbering, etc. are needed only to give intelligibility to detailed flow charts.

The detailed blow-by-blow flow chart, however, is an obsolete nuisance, suitable only for initiating beginners into algorithmic thinking. When introduced by Goldstine and von Neumann,[1] the little boxes and their contents served as a high-level language, grouping the inscrutable machine-language statements into clusters of significance. As Iverson early recognized,[2] in a systematic high-level language the clustering is already done, and each box contains a statement (Fig. 15.2). Then the boxes themselves become no more than a tedious and space-hogging exercise in drafting; they might as well be eliminated. Then nothing is left but the arrows. The arrows joining a statement to its successor are redundant; erase them. That leaves only GO TO's. And if one follows good practice and uses block structure to minimize GO TO's, there aren't many arrows, but they aid comprehension immensely. One might as well draw them on the listing and eliminate the flow chart altogether.

In fact, flow charting is more preached than practiced. I have never seen an experienced programmer who routinely made detailed flow charts before beginning to write programs. Where organization standards require flow charts, these are almost invariably done after the fact. Many shops proudly use machine programs to generate this "indispensable design tool" from the completed code. I think this universal experience is not an embarrassing and deplorable departure from good practice, to be acknowledged only with a nervous laugh. Instead it is the application of good judgment, and it teaches us something about the utility of flow charts.

The Apostle Peter said of new Gentile converts and the Jewish law, "Why lay a load on [their] backs which neither our ancestors nor we ourselves were able to carry?" (Acts 15:10, TEV). I would say the same about new programmers and the obsolete practice of flow charting.

Self-Documenting Programs

A basic principle of data processing teaches the folly of trying to maintain independent files in synchronism. It is far better to combine them into one file with each record containing all the information both files held concerning a given key.

Yet our practice in programming documentation violates our own teaching. We typically attempt to maintain a machine-readable form of a program and an independent set of human-readable documentation, consisting of prose and flow charts.

The results in fact confirm our teachings about the folly of separate files. Program documentation is notoriously poor, and its maintenance is worse. Changes made in the program do not promptly, accurately, and invariably appear in the paper.

The solution, I think, is to merge the files, to incorporate the documentation in the source program. This is at once a powerful incentive toward proper maintenance, and an insurance that the documentation will always be handy to the program user. Such programs are called *self-documenting*.

Now clearly this is awkward (but not impossible) if flow charts are to be included. But grant the obsolescence of flow charts and the dominant use of high-level language, and it becomes reasonable to combine the program and the documentation.

The use of a source program as a documentation medium imposes some constraints. On the other hand, the intimate availability of the source program, line by line, to the reader of the documentation makes possible new techniques. The time has

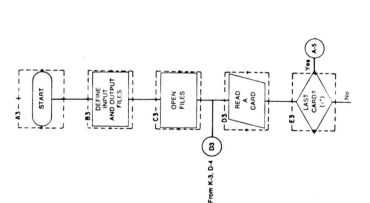

```
PGM6: PROCEDURE OPTIONS (MAIN);

    DECLARE SALEFL FILE
        RECORD
        INPUT
        ENVIRONMENT (F(80) MEDIUM (SYSIPT, 250));
    DECLARE PRINT4 FILE
        RECORD
        OUTPUT
        ENVIRONMENT (F(132) MEDIUM (SYSLST,1403) CTLASA);
    DECLARE 01 SALESCARD,
        03 BLANK1          CHARACTER (9);
        03 SALESNUM        PICTURE '9999';
        03 NAME            CHARACTER (25);
        03 BLANK2          CHARACTER (7);
        03 CURRENT_SALES   PICTURE '9999V99';
        03 BLANK3          CHARACTER (29);
    DECLARE 01 SALESLIST,
        03 CONTROL         CHARACTER (1) INITIAL (' ');
        03 SALESNUM_OUT    PICTURE 'ZZZ9';
        03 FILLER1         CHARACTER (5) INITIAL (' ');
        03 NAME_OUT        CHARACTER (25);
        03 FILLER2         CHARACTER (5) INITIAL (' ');
        03 CURRENT_OUT     PICTURE 'Z,ZZZV.99';
        03 FILLER3         CHARACTER (5) INITIAL (' ');
        03 PERCENT         PICTURE 'Z9';
        03 SIGN            CHARACTER (1) INITIAL ('%');
        03 FILLER4         CHARACTER (5) INITIAL (' ');
        03 COMMISSION      PICTURE 'Z,ZZZV.99';
        03 FILLER5         CHARACTER (63) INITIAL (' ');

OPEN FILE (SALEFL),FILE (PRINT4);

ON ENDFILE (SALEFL) GO TO ENDOFJOB;
```

Flowchart:

A3 — START

B3 — DEFINE INPUT AND OUTPUT FILES

C3 — OPEN FILES

From K-3, D-4 → D3

D3 — READ A CARD

E3 — LAST CARD? (/') — Yes → A-5 — No

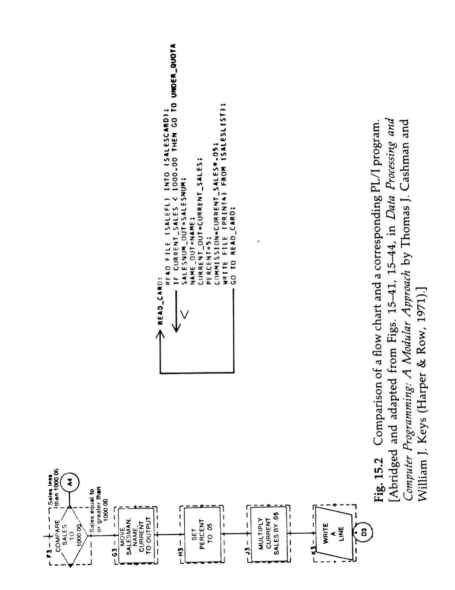

Fig. 15.2 Comparison of a flow chart and a corresponding PL/I program. [Abridged and adapted from Figs. 15–41, 15–44, in *Data Processing and Computer Programming: A Modular Approach* by Thomas J. Cashman and William J. Keys (Harper & Row, 1971).]

come to devise radically new approaches and methods for program documentation.

As a principal objective, we must attempt to minimize the burden of documentation, the burden neither we nor our predecessors have been able to bear successfully.

An approach. The first notion is to use the parts of the program that have to be there anyway, for programming language reasons, to carry as much of the documentation as possible. So labels, declaration statements, and symbolic names are all harnessed to the task of conveying as much meaning as possible to the reader.

A second notion is to use space and format as much as possible to improve readability and show subordination and nesting.

The third notion is to insert the necessary prose documentation into the program as paragraphs of comment. Most programs tend to have enough line-by-line comments; those programs produced to meet stiff organizational standards for "good documentation" often have too many. Even these programs, however, are usually deficient in the paragraph comments that really give intelligibility and overview to the whole thing.

Since the documentation is built into the structure, naming, and formats of the program, much of it *must* be done when the program is first written. But that is when it *should* be written. Since the self-documentation approach minimizes extra work, there are fewer obstacles to doing it then.

Some techniques. Figure 15.3 shows a self-documenting PL/I program.[3] The numbers in the circles are not part of it; they are meta-documentation keyed to the discussion.

1. Use a separate job name for each run, and maintain a run log showing what was tried, when, and the results. If the name is composed of a mnemonic part (here *QLT*) and a numerical suffix (here *4*), the suffix can be used as a run number, tying listings and log together. This technique requires a new job card for each run, but they can be made up in batches, duplicating the common information.

Fig. 15.3 A self-documenting program. ⟶

```
① //QLT4 JOB ...

② QLTSRT7: PROCEDURE (V);

    /**********************************************************************/
③   /*A SORT SUBROUTINE FOR 2500 6-BYTE FIELDS, PASSED AS THE VECTOR V.   A  */
    /*SEPARATELY COMPILED, NOT-MAIN PROCEDURE, WHICH MUST USE AUTOMATIC CORE */
    /*ALLOCATION.                                                         */
    /*                                                                    */
④   /*THE SORT ALGORITHM FOLLOWS BROOKS AND IVERSON, AUTOMATIC DATA PROCESSING,*/
    /*PROGRAM 7.23, P. 350.  THAT ALGORITHM IS REVISED AS FOLLOWS:        */
⑤   /*  STEPS 2-12 ARE SIMPLIFIED FOR M=2.                                */
    /*  STEP 18 IS EXPANDED TO HANDLE EXPLICIT INDEXING OF THE OUTPUT VECTOR. */
    /*  THE WHOLE FIELD IS USED AS THE SORT KEY.                          */
    /*  MINUS INFINITY IS REPRESENTED BY ZEROS.                           */
    /*  PLUS INFINITY IS REPRESENTED BY ONES.                             */
    /*  THE STATEMENT NUMBERS IN PROG. 7.23 ARE REFLECTED IN THE STATEMENT  */
    /*    LABELS OF THIS PROGRAM.                                         */
    /*  AN IF-THEN-ELSE CONSTRUCTION REQUIRES REPETITION OF A FEW LINES.  */
    /*                                                                    */
    /*TO CHANGE THE DIMENSION OF THE VECTOR TO BE SORTED, ALWAYS CHANGE THE  */
    /*INITIALIZATION OF T.  IF THE SIZE EXCEEDS 4096, CHANGE THE SIZE OF T,TOO.*/
    /*A MORE GENERAL VERSION WOULD PARAMETERIZE THE DIMENSION OF V.       */
    /*                                                                    */
    /*THE PASSED INPUT VECTOR IS REPLACED BY THE REORDERED OUTPUT VECTOR. */
    /**********************************************************************/

⑥  /* LEGEND   (ZERO-ORIGIN INDEXING)                                    */

    DECLARE
    (H,                     /*INDEX FOR INITIALIZING T                   */
     I,                     /*INDEX OF ITEM TO BE REPLACED               */
     J,                     /*INITIAL INDEX OF BRANCHES FROM NODE I      */
     K) BINARY FIXED,       /*INDEX IN OUTPUT VECTOR                     */

    (MINF,                  /*MINUS INFINITY                             */
     PINF) BIT (48),        /*PLUS INFINITY                              */

     V (*)   BIT (*),       /*PASSED VECTOR TO BE SORTED AND RETURNED    */

     T (0:8190) BIT (48);   /*WORKSPACE CONSISTING OF VECTOR TO BE SORTED, FILLED*/
                            /*OUT WITH INFINITIES, PRECEDED BY LOWER LEVELS  */
                            /*FILLED UP WITH MINUS INFINITIES            */

    /* NOW INITIALIZATION TO FILL DUMMY LEVELS, TOP LEVEL, AND UNUSED PART OF TOP*/
    /* LEVEL AS REQUIRED.                                                 */

⑦ INIT: MINF= (48) '0'B;
        PINF= (48) '1'B;

        DO L=  0 TO 4094;  T(L) = MINF;       END;
        DO L=  0 TO 2499;  T(L+4095) = V(L);  END;
        DO L=6595 TO 8190; T(L) = PINF;       END;

⑧ K0:   K = -1;
  K1:   I = 0;                /*                                    <------|  */
  K3:   J = 2*I+1;            /*SET J TO SCAN BRANCHES FROM NODE I.  <-----||  */
  K7:   IF T(J) <= T(J+1)     /*PICK SMALLER BRANCH                  __>__||  */
          THEN                /*                                         |||  */
⑨        DO;                  /*                                         |||  */
  K11:      T(I) = T(J);  /*REPLACE                                      |||  */
  K13:      IF T(I) = PINF THEN GO TO K16; /*IF INFINITY, REPLACEMENT_+∞__|||  */
                              /* IS FINISHED                            ||||  */
  K12:      I = J;            /*SET INDEX FOR HIGHER LEVEL              ||||  */
          END;                /*                                  <---+-||  */
          ELSE                /*                                      | |||  */
          DO;                 /*                                      | |||  */
  K11A:     T(I) = T(J+1);  /*                                        +∞ ||| */
  K13A:     IF T(I) = PINF THEN GO TO K16;      /*                 _+∞__|||  */
  K12A:     I = J+1;          /*                                       | |||  */
          END;                /*                                     < | |||  */
  K14:  IF 2*I < 8191 THEN GO TO K3;  /*GO BACK IF NOT ON TOP LEVEL ----+-||  */
  K15:  T(I) = PINF;   /*IF TOP LEVEL, FILL WITH INFINITY                 ||  */
  K16:  IF T(0) = PINF THEN RETURN;   /*TEST END OF SORT          <---|  |  */
  K17:  IF T(0) = MINF THEN GO TO K1; /*FLUSH OUT INITIAL DUMMIES _-∞____|  */
  K18:  K = K+1;                      /*STEP STORAGE INDEX                */
        V(K) = T(0);  GO TO K1;       /*STORE OUTPUT ITEM          -------|  */
  END QLTSRT7;
```

2. Use a program name that is mnemonic but also contains a version identifier. That is, assume there will be several versions. Here the index is the low order digit of the year 1967.

3. Incorporate the prose description as comments to PROCE-DURE.

4. Refer to standard literature to document basic algorithms wherever possible. This saves space, usually points to a much fuller treatment than one would provide, and allows the knowledgeable reader to skip it with confidence that he understands you.

5. Show the relationship to the book algorithm:
   a) changes   b) specialization   c) representation

6. Declare all variables. Use mnemonic names. Use comments to convert DECLARE into a complete legend. Note that it already contains names and structural descriptions, it needs only to be augmented with descriptions of *purpose*. By doing so here, one can avoid repeating the names and structural descriptions in a separate treatment.

7. Mark the initialization by a label.

8. Label statements in groups to show correspondences to the statements in the algorithm description in the literature.

9. Use indenting to show structure and grouping.

10. Add logical flow arrows to the listing by hand. They are very helpful in debugging and changing. They may be incorporated in the right margin of the comments space, and made part of the machine-readable text.

11. Use line comments or remark anything that is not obvious. If the techniques above have been used, these will be short and fewer in number than is customary.

12. Put multiple statements on one line, or one statement on several lines to match thought-grouping and to show correspondence to other algorithm description.

Why not?   What are the drawbacks of such an approach to documentation? There are several, which have been real but are becoming imaginary with changing times.

The most serious objection is the increase in the size of the source code that must be stored. As the discipline moves more and more toward on-line storage of source code, this has become a growing consideration. I find myself being briefer in comments to an APL program, which will live on a disk, than on a PL/I one that I will store as cards.

Yet simultaneously we are moving also toward on-line storage of prose documents for access and for updating via computerized text-editing. As shown above, amalgamating prose and program *reduces* the total number of characters to be stored.

A similar answer applies to the argument that self-documenting programs require more keystrokes. A typed document requires at least one keystroke per character per draft. A self-documenting program has fewer total characters and also fewer strokes per character, since drafts aren't retyped.

How about flow charts and structure graphs? If one uses only a highest-level structure graph, it might safely be kept as a separate document, for it is not subject to frequent change. But it can certainly be incorporated into the source program as a comment, and that seems wise.

To what extent are the techniques used above applicable to assembly language programs? I think the basic approach of self-documentation is thoroughly applicable. Space and formats are less free, and thus cannot be so flexibly used. Names and structural declarations can surely be exploited. Macros can help a great deal. The extensive use of paragraph comments is good practice in any language.

But the self-documentation approach is stimulated by the use of high-level languages and finds its greatest power and its greatest justification in high-level languages used with on-line systems, whether batch or interactive. As I have argued, such languages and systems help programmers in very powerful ways. Since machines are made for people, not people for machines, their use makes every form of sense, economic and human.

Epilogue

The tar pit of software engineering will continue to be sticky for a long time to come. One can expect the human race to continue attempting systems just within or just beyond our reach; and software systems are perhaps the most intricate and complex of man's handiworks. The management of this complex craft will demand our best use of new languages and systems, our best adaptation of proven engineering management methods, liberal doses of common sense, and a God-given humility to recognize our fallibility and limitations.

Notes and References

Chapter 1

1. Ershov considers this not only a woe, but also a part of the joy. A. P. Ershov, "Aesthetics and the human factor in programming," *CACM*, **15**, 7 (July, 1972), pp. 501–505.

Chapter 2

1. V.A. Vyssotsky of Bell Telephone Laboratories estimates that a large project can sustain a manpower buildup of 30 percent per year. More than that strains and even inhibits the evolution of the essential informal structure and its communication pathways discussed in Chapter 7.
   F. J. Corbató of MIT points out that a long project must anticipate a turnover of 20 percent per year, and these must be both technically trained and integrated into the formal structure.

2. C. Portman of International Computers Limited says, *"When everything has been seen to work, all integrated, you have four more months work to do."* Several other sets of schedule divisions are given in Wolverton, R. W., "The cost of developing large-scale software," *IEEE Trans. on Computers*, **C-23**, 6 (June, 1974) pp. 615–636.

3. Figures 2.5 through 2.8 are due to Jerry Ogdin, who in quoting my example from an earlier publication of this chapter much improved its illustration. Ogdin, J. L., "The Mongolian hordes versus superprogrammer," *Infosystems* (December, 1972), pp. 20–23.

Chapter 3

1. Sackman, H., W. J. Erikson, and E. E. Grant, "Exploratory experimental studies comparing online and offline programming performance," *CACM,* **11,** 1 (January, 1968), pp. 3–11.

2. Mills, H., "Chief programmer teams, principles, and procedures," IBM Federal Systems Division Report FSC 71–5108, Gaithersburg, Md., 1971.

3. Baker, F. T., "Chief programmer team management of production programming," *IBM Sys. J.,* **11,** 1 (1972).

Chapter 4

1. Eschapasse, M., *Reims Cathedral,* Caisse Nationale des Monuments Historiques, Paris, 1967.

2. Brooks, F. P., "Architectural philosophy," in W. Buchholz (ed.), *Planning A Computer System.* New York: McGraw-Hill, 1962.

3. Blaauw, G. A., "Hardware requirements for the fourth generation," in F. Gruenberger (ed.), *Fourth Generation Computers.* Englewood Cliffs, N.J.: Prentice-Hall, 1970.

4. Brooks, F. P., and K. E. Iverson, *Automatic Data Processing, System/360 Edition.* New York: Wiley, 1969, Chapter 5.

5. Glegg, G. L., *The Design of Design.* Cambridge: Cambridge Univ. Press, 1969, says *"At first sight, the idea of any rules or principles being superimposed on the creative mind seems more likely to hinder than to help, but this is quite untrue in practice. Disciplined thinking focusses inspiration rather than blinkers it."*

6. Conway, R. W., "The PL/C Compiler," *Proceedings of a Conf. on Definition and Implementation of Universal Programming Languages.* Stuttgart, 1970.

7. For a good discussion of the necessity for programming technology, see C. H. Reynolds, "What's wrong with computer

programming management?" in G. F. Weinwurm (ed.), *On the Management of Computer Programming.* Philadelphia: Auerbach, 1971, pp. 35–42.

Chapter 5

1. Strachey, C., "Review of *Planning a Computer System,*" *Comp. J.,* **5,** 2 (July, 1962), pp. 152–153.

2. This applies only to the control programs. Some of the compiler teams in the OS/360 effort were building their third or fourth systems, and the excellence of their products shows it.

3. Shell, D. L., "The Share 709 system: a cooperative effort"; Greenwald, I. D., and M. Kane, "The Share 709 system: programming and modification"; Boehm, E. M., and T. B. Steel, Jr., "The Share 709 system: machine implementation of symbolic programming"; all in *JACM,* **6,** 2 (April, 1959), pp. 123–140.

Chapter 6

1. Neustadt, R. E., *Presidential Power.* New York: Wiley, 1960, Chapter 2.

2. Backus, J. W., "The syntax and semantics of the proposed international algebraic language." *Proc. Intl. Conf. Inf. Proc. UNESCO,* Paris, 1959, published by R. Oldenbourg, Munich, and Butterworth, London. Besides this, a whole collection of papers on the subject is contained in T.B. Steel, Jr. (ed.), *Formal Language Description Languages for Computer Programming.* Amsterdam: North Holland, (1966).

3. Lucas, P., and K. Walk, "On the formal description of PL/I," *Annual Review in Automatic Programming Language.* New York: Wiley, 1962, Chapter 2, p. 2.

4. Iverson, K. E., *A Programming Language.* New York: Wiley, 1962, Chapter 2.

5. Falkoff, A. D., K. E. Iverson, E. H. Sussenguth, "A formal description of System/360," *IBM Systems Journal,* **3,** 3 (1964), pp. 198–261.

6. Bell, C. G., and A. Newell, *Computer Structures.* New York: McGraw-Hill, 1970, pp. 120–136, 517–541.

7. Bell, C. G., private communication.

Chapter 7

1. Parnas, D. L., "Information distribution aspects of design methodology," Carnegie-Mellon Univ., Dept. of Computer Science Technical Report, February, 1971.

2. Heinlein, R. A., *The Man Who Sold the Moon.* New York: Signet, 1951, pp. 103–104. Reprinted by permission of the author, copyright 1950 by Robert A. Heinlein.

Chapter 8

1. Sackman, H., W. J. Erikson, and E. E. Grant, "Exploratory experimentation studies comparing online and offline programming performance," *CACM,* **11,** 1 (January, 1968), pp. 3–11.

2. Nanus, B., and L. Farr, "Some cost contributors to large-scale programs," *AFIPS Proc. SJCC,* **25** (Spring, 1964), pp. 239–248.

3. Weinwurm, G. F., "Research in the management of computer programming," Report SP-2059, System Development Corp., Santa Monica, 1965.

4. Morin, L. H., "Estimation of resources for computer programming projects," M. S. thesis, Univ. of North Carolina, Chapel Hill, 1974.

5. Portman, C., private communication.

6. An unpublished 1964 study by E. F. Bardain shows programmers realizing 27 percent productive time. (Quoted by D.B.

Mayer and A. W. Stalnaker, "Selection and evaluation of computer personnel," *Proc. 23rd ACM Conf.,* 1968, p. 661.)

7. Aron, J., private communication.

8. Paper given at a panel session and not included in the *AFIPS Proceedings.*

9. Wolverton, R. W., "The cost of developing large-scale software," *IEEE Trans. on Computers,* **C-23,** 6 (June, 1974) pp. 615–636. This important recent paper contains data on many of the issues of this chapter, as well as confirming the productivity conclusions.

10. Corbató, F. J., "Sensitive issues in the design of multi-use systems," lecture at the opening of the Honeywell EDP Technology Center, 1968.

11. W. M. Taliaffero also reports a constant productivity of 2400 statements/year in assembler, Fortran, and Cobol. See "Modularity. The key to system growth potential," *Software,* **1,** 3 (July 1971) pp. 245–257.

12. E. A. Nelson's System Development Corp. Report TM-3225, *Management Handbook for the Estimation of Computer Programming Costs,* shows a 3-to-1 productivity improvement for high-level language (pp. 66–67), although his standard deviations are wide.

Chapter 9

1. Brooks, F. P. and K. E. Iverson, *Automatic Data Processing, System/360 Edition.* New York: Wiley, 1969, Chapter 6.

2. Knuth, D. E., *The Art of Computer Programming,* Vols. 1–3. Reading, Mass.: Addison-Wesley, 1968, ff.

Chapter 10

1. Conway, M. E., "How do committees invent?" *Datamation,* **14,** 4 (April, 1968), pp. 28–31.

Chapter 11

1. Speech at Oglethorpe University, May 22, 1932.

2. An illuminating account of Multics experience on two successive systems is in F. J. Corbató, J. H. Saltzer, and C. T. Clingen, "Multics—the first seven years," *AFIPS Proc SJCC,* **40** (1972), pp. 571–583.

3. Cosgrove, J., "Needed: a new planning framework," *Datamation,* **17,** 23 (Dec., 1971), pp. 37–39.

4. The matter of design change is complex, and I oversimplify here. See J. H. Saltzer, "Evolutionary design of complex systems," in D. Eckman (ed.), *Systems: Research and Design.* New York: Wiley, 1961. When all is said and done, however, I still advocate building a pilot system whose discarding is planned.

5. Campbell, E., "Report to the AEC Computer Information Meeting," December, 1970. The phenomenon is also discussed by J. L. Ogdin in "Designing reliable software," *Datamation,* **18,** 7 (July, 1972), pp. 71–78. My experienced friends seem divided rather evenly as to whether the curve finally goes down again.

6. Lehman, M., and L. Belady, "Programming system dynamics," given at the ACM SIGOPS Third Symposium on Operating System Principles, October, 1971.

7. Lewis, C. S., *Mere Christianity.* New York: Macmillan, 1960, p. 54.

Chapter 12

1. See also J. W. Pomeroy, "A guide to programming tools and techniques," *IBM Sys. J.,* **11,** 3 (1972), pp. 234–254.

2. Landy, B., and R. M. Needham, "Software engineering techniques used in the development of the Cambridge Multiple-Access System," *Software,* **1,** 2 (April, 1971), pp. 167–173.

3. Corbató, F. J., "PL/I as a tool for system programming," *Datamation*, **15,** 5 (May, 1969), pp. 68–76.

4. Hopkins, M., "Problems of PL/I for system programming," IBM Research Report RC 3489, Yorktown Heights, N.Y., August 5, 1971.

5. Corbató, F. J., J. H. Saltzer, and C. T. Clingen, "Multics—the first seven years," *AFIPS Proc SJCC,* **40** (1972), pp. 571–582. *"Only a half-dozen areas which were written in PL/I have been recoded in machine language for reasons of squeezing out the utmost in performance. Several programs, originally in machine language, have been recoded in PL/I to increase their maintainability."*

6. To quote Corbató's paper cited in reference 3: *"PL/I is here now and the alternatives are still untested."* But see a quite contrary view, well-documented, in Henricksen, J. O. and R. E. Merwin, "Programming language efficiency in real-time software systems," *AFIPS Proc SJCC,* **40** (1972) pp. 155–161.

7. Not all agree. Harlan Mills says, in a private communication, *"My experience begins to tell me that in production programming the person to put at the terminal is the secretary. The idea is to make programming a more public practice, under common scrutiny of many team members, rather than a private art."*

8. Harr, J., "Programming Experience for the Number 1 Electronic Switching System," paper given at the 1969 SJCC.

Chapter 13

1. Vyssotsky, V. A., "Common sense in designing testable software," lecture at The Computer Program Test Methods Symposium, Chapel Hill, N.C., 1972. Most of Vyssotsky's lecture is contained in Hetzel, W. C. (ed.), *Program Test Methods.* Englewood Cliffs, N.J.: Prentice-Hall, 1972, pp. 41–47.

2. Wirth, N., "Program development by stepwise refinement," *CACM* **14,** 4 (April, 1971), pp. 221–227. See also Mills, H. "Top-down programming in large systems," in R. Rustin (ed.). *Debugging Techniques in Large Systems.* Englewood Cliffs, N.J.: Prentice-Hall, 1971, pp. 41–55 and Baker, F. T., "System quality through structured programming," *AFIPS Proc FJCC,* **41-I** (1972), pp. 339–343.

3. Dahl, O. J., E. W. Dijkstra, and C. A. R. Hoare, *Structured Programming.* London and New York: Academic Press, 1972. This volume contains the fullest treatment. See also Dijkstra's germinal letter, "GOTO statement considered harmful," *CACM,* **11,** 3 (March, 1968), pp. 147–148.

4. Böhm, C., and A. Jacopini, "Flow diagrams, Turing machines, and languages with only two formation rules," *CACM,* **9,** 5 (May, 1966), pp. 366–371.

5. Codd, E. F., E. S. Lowry, E. McDonough, and C. A. Scalzi, "Multiprogramming STRETCH: Feasibility considerations," *CACM,* **2,** 11 (Nov., 1959), pp. 13–17.

6. Strachey, C., "Time sharing in large fast computers," *Proc. Int. Conf. on Info. Processing,* UNESCO (June, 1959), pp. 336–341. See also Codd's remarks on p. 341, where he reported progress on work like that proposed in Strachey's paper.

7. Corbató, F. J., M. Merwin-Daggett, R. C. Daley, "An experimental time-sharing system," *AFIPS Proc. SJCC,* **2,** (1962), pp. 335–344. Reprinted in S. Rosen, *Programming Systems and Languages.* New York: McGraw-Hill, 1967, pp. 683–698.

8. Gold, M. M., "A methodology for evaluating time-shared computer system usage," Ph.D. dissertation, Carnegie-Mellon University, 1967, p. 100.

9. Gruenberger, F., "Program testing and validating," *Datamation,* **14,** 7, (July, 1968), pp. 39–47.

10. Ralston, A., *Introduction to Programming and Computer Science.* New York: McGraw-Hill, 1971, pp. 237–244.

11. Brooks, F. P., and K. E. Iverson, *Automatic Data Processing, System/360 Edition.* New York: Wiley, 1969, pp. 296–299.

12. A good treatment of development of specifications and of system build and test is given by F. M. Trapnell, "A systematic approach to the development of system programs," *AFIPS Proc SJCC,* **34** (1969) pp. 411–418.

13. A real-time system will require an environment simulator. See, for example, M. G. Ginzberg, "Notes on testing real-time system programs," *IBM Sys. J.,* **4,** 1 (1965), pp. 58–72.

14. Lehman, M., and L. Belady, "Programming system dynamics," given at the ACM SIGOPS Third Symposium on Operating System Principles, October, 1971.

Chapter 14

1. See C. H. Reynolds, "What's wrong with computer programming management?" in G. F. Weinwurm (ed.), *On the Management of Computer Programming.* Philadelphia: Auerbach, 1971, pp. 35–42.

2. King, W. R., and T. A. Wilson, "Subjective time estimates in critical path planning—a preliminary analysis," *Mgt. Sci.,* **13,** 5 (Jan., 1967), pp. 307–320, and sequel, W. R. King, D. M. Witterrongel, K. D. Hezel, "On the analysis of critical path time estimating behavior," *Mgt. Sci.,* **14,** 1 (Sept., 1967), pp. 79–84.

3. For a fuller discussion, see Brooks, F. P., and K. E. Iverson, *Automatic Data Processing, System/360 Edition,* New York: Wiley, 1969, pp. 428–430.

4. Private communication.

Chapter 15

1. Goldstine, H. H., and J. von Neumann, "Planning and coding problems for an electronic computing instrument," Part II, Vol. 1, report prepared for the U.S. Army Ordinance Department, 1947; reprinted in J. von Neumann, *Collected Works*, A. H. Taub (ed.), Vol. v., New York: McMillan, pp. 80–151.

2. Private communication, 1957. The argument is published in Iverson, K. E., "The Use of APL in Teaching," Yorktown, N.Y.: IBM Corp., 1969.

3. Another list of techniques for PL/I is given by A. B. Walter and M. Bohl in "From better to best—tips for good programming," *Software Age,* **3,** 11 (Nov., 1969), pp. 46–50.

   The same techniques can be used in Algol and even Fortran. D. E. Lang of the University of Colorado has a Fortran formatting program called STYLE that accomplishes such a result. See also D. D. McCracken and G. M. Weinberg, "How to write a readable FORTRAN program," *Datamation,* **18,** 10 (Oct., 1972), pp. 73–77.

Index

Note: Bold numerals indicate relatively substantial discussions of a topic.